The Virgin Widow

For those who seek sense and solace in a time of sorrow.

ANDREA S. GOULD PH.D.

ISBN-10:   0615636268
EAN-13:   9780615636269

Library of Congress Control Number: 2012938623
CreateSpace, North Charleston, SC

Contents

Acknowledgements

As all things are interconnected, this writing came to fruition as another link in a long chain of events, reactions and reflections beginning with my lifelong habit of journal keeping, a practice that has kept me learning and growing throughout life's constant convolutions. My firm belief in this habit helped me turn the experience of loss into a guide for those who find themselves on a similar path.

My gratitude goes first to those who believed in my ability to connect the words in my heart with the souls of others. To Richard, my late husband, the stimulus for this work, with deep appreciation for his undying faith in me. He continues to be an invisible wind beneath my wings as I navigate the rich and complex territory of my ever-evolving life.

To my stepchildren, Jason and Jennifer, whose lives continue to echo and embody their father's devotion to the next generation.

To my son, Alexander, and his wife, Virginia Kathleen, who have already demonstrated an amazing ability to overcome adversity in their young lives.

To Ruth and Frank Gould, my parents, who intuitively knew since my childhood that I would someday write to soothe, serve and offer counsel to those in need.

To Gail Grossman, my dear friend and confidant, who left us all too soon and whose humor, judgment, and support live within me as sustenance everlasting.

To my clients, whose life stories and profound trust in me prepared the soil for all that springs forth as wisdom to be shared.

To my dear friends , whose love and encouragement, chiding, and teasing maintain persistent faith in my contributions. Thank you, Carol Markman, Robbie Glantz, Diane Kramer, Karen Wexler Berry, Shelley Friedman, Arlene Haims, and Rosanne Scarpelli.

To my young assistant, Elizabeth Quarles, whose curiosity and intelligence has always motivated me as I made the long uphill climb toward completing this book.

To my writing group who encouraged the nascent efforts of turning my voluminous journals into a guidebook for people who have lost a significant other. Thank you, Joan Campagna, Liza Johnson, and Jean Brown for your loving guidance and grace on the long road from 'then' to 'now.'

Deepest gratitude goes to Abby Hagyard, whose wise editing, comic companionship, and commitment to compassionate criticism extended the necessary

Acknowledgements

reach into the depths of my psyche. Our writing sessions offered smart sensitivity, as she wove a crystalline cocoon around this difficult material, midwifing it into a form that you, dear readers, could readily digest.

And to Michael Wm. Marks, who lovingly led me to the promised land of my new home, offering me the safety and sanctuary to complete this work.

Dear Reader...

It is within the context of death that life takes on its vivid nature.

The Virgin Widow is my story, but it is yours as well. Like you, and like millions of other women, I became a "Virgin Widow" overnight. Like you, I willed myself to survive.

As a psychologist, I am sensitive to the shades of psychic change. I have always found writing to be a way of helping me to digest and understand my experiences. Even as I mourned my loss, my journal entries became a reflection on the process of adjusting to change and transition itself. This book, therefore, is both a memoir and a personal-growth book for individuals like you who have recently lost a partner. My 'notes from the front' are meant to guide you on your own healing path.

When the reality of losing a partner is thrust upon us, we are often unprepared. The grief that accompanies the loss can be overwhelming. Not only do we mourn the comfort and the familiarity of our partner, but we also find ourselves being forced into a new, unwelcome, and radically shifted world-picture that eerily—frustratingly—contains many of the same objects, people, and places, although we see these in a different light.

By my definition, "Virgin Widows" are innocent, first-time widows. They have no experience from which to draw the wisdom, philosophy, and behavior necessary to find a way through the intricate and immobilizing situations demanding their attention. Though they may have loved and lost before, they have never experienced the absolute finality that the death of their loved one imposes on their world.

Whether a loss is a "complicated" grief — when death is the result of unusual circumstances: accident, suicide, or mayhem—or the natural outcome of a long and happy life, pain, uncertainty, and the need for guided healing are no less diminished.

I have been trained to be both an observer and experiencer, creating for myself and others a delicate balance, between who we are and who and what we are to become. As I worked through my own grief and began to rebuild in the days and months following my husband's death, the liberating gift of my professional training gave me permission to reclaim control of my life. I intend to help you do the same as I share my thoughts with you.

Losing a spouse carries with it the loss of life as planned. Coupled life carries with it a shared identity, so this identity is lost too. We lose our friend, our lover, and our partner. The ultimate crippling blow comes when we realize that we have lost an essential part of ourselves as well. And because it takes time for the reinvention process to begin, we can do little more than face each day, one day at a time, under a magnifying glass, in a kind of self-imposed exile.

The time to reinvent ourselves does come, however, and when it does, we know what it is to crave normalcy, to have some semblance of our original self returned to us, to seek the ordinary comforts of companionship, and to feel the first stirrings of curiosity about our desirability: "Will I ever love again?" and "Will anyone again love me for me?"

This is the start of the healing process. Though conventional wisdom says that new partnerships are not the way to soothe our loss, we are social beings who grow and change through our interactions. Balanced against those times of much-needed, sacred solitude is a loving network of friends and family, and it works as an incubator, nurturing and protecting us while we reconfigure our newly evolving selves.

For me, "staying in the present" was of primary importance, both as a safety zone between the poignancy of a lost past and the frightening uncertainty of an abstract future. Though I was sometimes tempted to numb myself, I chose not to. My mind and body — trained by childbirth and sustained by meditation — acknowledged the intensity completely without shutting down.

For many months, it seemed that time hung suspended and that the happy and productive life I had known before my marriage and during the many years we shared our lives had been overshadowed by the Yesterday when he died and the endless Today in which I now lived. Moving in slow motion, I anchored my awareness to the spectrum of sensation and sanctuary that each moment offered.

Other times, I felt an impatience to get away, to be free of this dreadful burden of sorrow. On those days, my body ached — not for him, not to turn back time, but to fast forward to the day when I would awaken from this nightmare. I craved the day when my step would quicken as it had before and I would be consumed once more with my passionate belief in endless possibility.

That my moods diverged so drastically might seem strange to some. But I had come to this man and, eventually, to this marriage at a pivotal time in my adult life.

For as long as I can remember, although I was a whimsical child who loved magic and mystery and fantasy, I had known that I would follow a professional path. At the age of twenty-five, I had completed my Ph.D. and had entered my chosen profession, secure in the knowledge that I was a respected member of a close-knit community.

A college romance led to an early marriage. I was eager to be a wife, mother, and career woman, and very quickly, my dream came true. Though my son and I have a special, enduring bond, the connection between my husband and me faded quickly, and we soon divorced.

At thirty–three I was a single mother with a thriving practice. My life was full, my friends were many and varied, and I was at peace with myself and had faith in what the future held.

And then I attended a professional conference. It was a last-minute decision, really. I remember that a colleague had implored me to travel to Washington

D.C. "Go, a change of pace will do you good, and you never know...you might meet someone." And we had laughed. Little did we know...

Though it sounds like a typical clichéd romance, the man I met at that event seemed in every way I could imagine to be my soul mate. We were perfect for each other with the exception of geography. We lived thousands of miles apart; he in the west, me in New York and neither of us could relocate.

We tried to make it work, but the reality was that his shared custody restrictions were as limiting as mine. It was bittersweet because one of the things I loved about him was his integrity and commitment – he simply couldn't abandon his children. What's more, he completely understood that nothing would induce me to leave my son.

When we decided to end our love affair I truly thought I would lose my mind. The despair I felt was beyond words. I had found that rarest kind of love that poets speak of, and I had needed to let it go and walk away. Knowing he felt the same was paradoxically a comfort and a complex, impossible tangle. Two hearts forever joined; forever broken.

Somehow, the days unfolded. Friends and family did their best. Though I buried myself in my work and cherished the time I spent with my son, every fiber of my being was utterly and completely shattered. Every nerve ending was numb. I could not and would not smile.

Life went on, of course. It always does. And I went to work and raised my child and found the strength to keep on keeping on. In time, my appetite for life returned and I found my curiosity and zest growing back in a whole new way.

Five years later, in a purely professional context, I met Richard, my future husband. He was highly respected, admired by his peers, much loved by his students, attractive, intelligent, charming, and compassionate. We collaborated well. We enjoyed each other's company. A relationship seemed possible. "But wait," a voice inside my head insisted, "he's not your type." (It can be troublesome how many people carry illusions about what defines a workable partnership.) So, I chose to move slowly and give myself the space to consider this new man with my expanding intuition. I began, gradually and completely, to change my view about what constituted a 'meaningful partnership'. Through our differences, our struggles revealed major insights about honesty and vulnerability, and these became our guiding forces. Eventually, I surrendered to the learning, and to the love I was offered.

It took four years before I saw that something deeper and more intimate was evolving. It took nine years before I was ready to put away my dream of that for-ever lost love of mine and say, "I do."

"Let me be your landing lights," Richard had said. "Let me be the one you turn to." His logic and per-sistence appealed to me.

And finally, I did. And we had a good life. While at times, our very public, committed-to-career-and-community kind of life stressed my more flamboy-ant 'gypsy' parts, somewhere within me I knew we'd find a way to allow our differences to enhance rather than divide.

We all have many personalities that live within each of us, and we do ourselves a disservice to ignore them — or worse deny their existence. And I wanted to be sure I did not do that to the 'gypsy' part of me, the part who dreams, who rebels against schedules, whose lyrical mind crafts poetry and song, and who resists consistency and craves novelty.

And that was why it took me so long to allow the merg-ing of our lives to happen. In time, I learned to let his strength be mine, and to seek that gentle shelter from life's storms. I learned to trust that he would always be there, because he'd said he would. And then he died.

His sudden death profoundly ruptured my life and lifestyle. I reeled in disorientation, and roiled in sadness, trying to find solid ground. And one day I came to realize that some kind of decision had been made for me; one over which I had no control. I had no choice but to accept it.

Oddly, an inner voice reassured me that this new reality would prove to be perversely freeing in its accelerating force—and this was a voice I would not and could not hear, at first.

What was I doing when I got the call? So many people want to know. I was working with a client. My assistant, who never interrupts a session, tapped on the door. She told me that my husband's secretary was on the phone and needed to speak to me. My hands and feet seemed to move in frozen slow motion; my own voice sounded disembodied. In response to my simple questions, the secretary's answers were cryptic. Richard had collapsed-nothing was clear, nothing was certain. All I knew was that I had to drive to the hospital immediately. Only then would the truth be revealed. I knew better than to press for more information.

"I'm sorry," I told my client. "There has been an emergency with my husband."

"Let me drive you," he said. "Let me help."

NO!

I'm sure I said "No thank you" though by now, in shock, I was on automatic pilot, polite and mechanical..

I had to go alone. I had to be alone. I had no idea what rush of emotions might overtake me: if I would cry, if I would become ill, if I would have to stop the car and beat the steering wheel and scream. All I knew was that whatever I might do, whatever random choices my body might make, the last thing I needed was a witness, an audience.

"No. Thank you."

Yes, I'm sure that's what I must have said.

My grieving process, as it unfolded, became a series of pragmatic as well as artistic choices. What I mean by 'artistic' in this context is more like "creative", in that I am aware that I have choices. For me, this is where spirituality comes in.

These choices provided the necessary energy that allowed me to learn, change, and grow. Dealing with the unfamiliar encouraged me to get out of my own way and begin to change the course of my life.

The loss of my husband sealed the loss of my past and my future. An unexpected death reminds us of the randomness that the universe can offer, and it became terribly necessary to notice signs, signals, and synchronicities. These "stars" helped me to navigate the apparent paradox of my random universe.

It is within the context of death that life takes on its vivid nature. The vitality that revealed itself to me was in direct contrast to the actual experience of being intimately connected with the cessation of a life.

Our personalities shape the drama of change and transition in our lives. The ways we negotiate new realities can shift from locking ourselves away to seeking new horizons. The ways we relate with others can create an unexpected force field in the midst of the tedious tasks of cleaning up and repairing the holocaust of death. The landscape of grief is as different as we are and as universal at the same time.

During the months of grief, I grew to believe that the grace surrounding me at this time offered a rare opportunity to make certain kinds of changes in my life. Readying myself for this momentous journey, I gathered nine conceptual tools for survival:

- Knowing that life has chapters.

- Knowing that nothing stays the same.

- Knowing that attachment breeds suffering.

- Knowing how to breathe as a way of managing pain and intensity.

- Knowing how to write in order to cope with overwhelming feelings.

- Exercising choice whenever possible.

- Being able to surrender to something larger than oneself when necessary.

- Knowing that change is another name for the necessary process of self-transformation.

- Understanding that managing transition is a learnable set of skills.

The Virgin Widow traces my journey of grief, transition, and change in the wake of my husband's sudden death. It is divided into chapters that address the crises that I faced — and that you will also face during your own journey of rebuilding and rebirth.

The brief summaries written as conversations with myself — 'internal monologues' designed to prepare you for the best and the worst to come — are meant to add nutritious nuggets that trigger welcome release and that enable you to reweave a life tapestry that has been torn by despair.

Journal entries are a montage of private thoughts combined with excerpts of letters and exchanges with neighbors, friends, family members, colleagues, and clients who bore witness to this vulnerable transition period in my life. While these entries speak directly to *my* experience, they also serve to address a universal theme, helping you to see reflections of your own challenges as you struggle to find your path.

"Dear Reader" comments close each chapter. These are designed to offer suggestions and insights you may wish to consider in light of your own discoveries as you move forward.

At the end of your journey, you will come to understand where this Virgin Widow arrived, what she came to embrace, and how she has chosen to live. It is my hope that the mechanisms of "choosing" and "creating" a life will shed light on your challenge and provide a blueprint for rebuilding after *"life as we knew it"* is replaced by *"life as we might envision it."*

From both perspectives- as a widow and as a psychologist- I have come to know that grief is timeless. The personal and sensitive nature of a memoir requires us to write authentically if this genre is to be helpful to others. It has taken ten years for me to allow this material to ripen and for me to achieve the perspective necessary to craft a book that satisfies my requirement for sharing my story and being of service.

With blessings on your journey.

Andrea Gould

Chapter 1

At Ground Zero:
Words While Walking Wounded

*There is no ticking clock, for
time as I know it stands still.*

Today I am a Virgin Widow.

*Though I have known heartbreak, I am an innocent in this
intimate brush with death.*

I am oddly objective, separate, and apart from the pain. All business, I am taking care of business. Hearing the news, driving to the hospital, telling the doctor, "Yes, I do need a moment alone with him."

Does it help me at all that I am trained in matters such as this? That I counsel people every day, that I help them find their place in the world? It does. Their stories resonate as I cope with the details, answer the questions, and make the decisions. Shock is a cushion that keeps me safe, alert, and focused on what must be done while grief waits in the wings.

I return home—eager for sanctuary, for silence. When I open the door, expecting quiet, blissful solitude, I am (surprise!) surrounded by family and friends. I am stunned and confused. How did they all get here? And when?

Though it has been many hours since I received the call, for me, it has been but a single moment—a time outside of time. Not for them, of course. As the hours passed, they reached out, made plans, and gathered to comfort me. Now, at their touch, in the rush of their grief, my own floodgates open. Strong only moments ago, I am suddenly weak; I cannot seem to catch my breath. This is my first glimpse of the ordeal that is coming...

And so I begin this journal as a way to cope. If I cannot pour out my heart as I once did, secure in the sanctuary that was my husband's love, I will have this. It will be my raft within a storm. Here, I can confide the turmoil that rages within. I can use journaling to begin the process of reweaving this life unraveled and unraveling, tossing and turning, in hope, in frustration, in joy, in despair.

March 9

I am called to the hospital and I drive there, disconnected from my actions, full of knowing. Tightening and tingling, my entire body is alive with a message too big to bear. A long-ago memory: that quickening of my body at my water breaking, just prior to childbirth. At that time, I knew that life would never be the same. Now, I know it again.

When I counsel clients on grief, I say, "With change, we have choice: We can believe, avoid, or deny." Suddenly, I am living these words. The psychologist in me knows that these choices lie before me as I drive to the hospital. The woman in me is thinking, *"This moment in time is a turning point."*

This unexpected rupture has cut into the ground of my experience sharply—so sharply that I can barely keep myself from going numb. But I don't want to go numb. Numbing only makes it worse because the next moment will require me to awaken again. Reawakening is too painful. I make a conscious decision and resist the reflex action. I tell myself: "Take it now, feel the pain, stay awake!"

All of my senses and every fiber of my being are extended in exquisite sensitivity. The truth is waiting for me. Only then will it become reality for me, for everyone.

Hospitals have special rooms designed specifically to reveal the truth, to communicate life-changing information. Rooms that have thick cinder-block walls that contain the energy from the jolt of transformation. Rooms with no room for distraction. Truth compactors where the truth has nowhere to go but inward and downward.

The sensations for which I stay present are disorienting. The message travels swiftly, birdlike, from the top of my head, down my spine, and through my throat, heart, abdomen...uninterrupted.

"Can you accept this?" the message asks me at each nexus.

"Yes" comes the reply.

Is this what acceptance feels like?

Such a big reality to integrate, and as I integrate it, I know why I can do this. On some level, it comes as no surprise.

"Almost all in a day's work," a voice inside me murmurs. "No judgment, just a fact of life. My life. The lives of my clients. All of our lives. All of life. No illusions. You know how life is. And this is it. Your turn."

"Your husband is dead," they say. "We're so sorry. We tried everything."

I stand there and accept it. All six or seven of the medical staff who have tended Richard are packed into that tiny room. They are so mournful and earnest; they tried their best. For me, it is sensory overload, but I do not faint. What else is there to do?

Although the devastation is enormous, I can absorb it because the other truth is that the relentless pressures of my husband's job created the collision course he had set for himself. I had always wondered if someone could literally work himself to death. Of course, he was stronger than ever, having had a bifurcated aortic valve in his heart "repaired" almost two years ago. Then again, maybe I knew too much about stress and its insidiousness. Some things I guess we'd rather *not* know.

I spend time with him. Alone with him. Talking with him, knowing he cannot hear, yet still believing that my thoughts and prayers reach him, somehow, somewhere.

For me, this is a time outside the ordinary constraints of time. There is no ticking clock, for time as I know it stands still. With effort, I meet with the doctors, listen to their words. I say and do the things that must be said and done.

I get in my car and head home. Home is sanctuary. Home is where I can lock the door and, alone at last, try to make sense of it all. Sanctuary is what I crave. It waits for me, mere steps away. But when I open the door, the house is full. No less than twenty of my friends and family have arrived and gathered. Shocked, I cannot integrate the reality of all these people in this odd day with me.

How? I wonder.

How did they know?

The children were thousands of miles away, yet here they are–my 22 year old son from Arizona, my stepson from Los Angeles, my stepdaughter from North Carolina!

How did they get here?

In the close circle of their love, their sorrow, and their concern, my control melts away. Suddenly, the tears flow and I am shattered. I cannot seem to catch my breath.

March 10

Widows wake up early. No surprise, really. Early-morning waking is a sign of anxiety. Feelings and thoughts do a little dance and wake us with their movement. The experience begs for resolve, for relief. It can lead to purposeful action or more anxiety. Better to choose *some* action than to fall prey to the kind of dead-end trap of feeling oneself slide into an abyss.

I realize that I've said this to countless clients over the years while watching many of them struggle with this pre-dawn dilemma. The irony is that I am standing in their shoes. Struggling. I know that I need to be doing *something* rather than nothing.

I'm casting about within myself, trying to find a way to stay conscious while death blows my life apart. The most reliable way I know how to stay present is to write. Writing has always been a way for me to digest the moment-to-moment reality of life. To slow life down. To have a better chance of putting my feet on solid ground, I reach for my journal.

There's something about the touch and feel of a pen in my hand and the comfort of the smooth and empty page that orients me. What I write is up to me. What I write is a living choice about how to represent what is happening to me. What I write is reflected back to me and represents what I ultimately feel. There is reciprocity here, a way of metabolizing the moments, like eating food and turning it into fuel. Writing turns experience into story. And story becomes feeling. I can control what I feel depending on how I write it. Aware of the need to control the uncontrollable, I write everything down. It's all I have.

I need a place to put myself. My writing is who I am. I write; therefore, I am. If I don't write, I don't exist.

Some things become obsessions when life is blown apart—and I require a new container for this larger-than-life experience. Even now, I sense that this will be an ongoing quest: to seek a container that is vast enough, strong enough, accepting enough.

What will I use to hold my thoughts and feelings together now, today? My eyes are caught by a beautiful painting on the cover of a blank book I've buried in my cache of attractive books for capturing my thoughts. This cover depicting a sleeping beauty of a woman on the forest floor speaks to the archetype of dormancy and transformation. My words enter this world with the relief of finding a verdant and temporary haven for my sorely fragmented self. I write with care…

The 9th of March

My life…forever changed.
By the passing
Of my husband
Suddenly and
Unexpectedly
On this last Tuesday morning
10:17AM
AT HIS DESK
At
His Beloved School, his place of work, his labor of love.

March 11

It's 1:25 a.m. I am afraid to sleep; afraid that if I dream, I will float into the comfortable memory of life "Before." I fear that my nervous system will send habitual messages to my dreaming self and that I'll awaken thinking he is still here. To revisit the hard-won truth seems unbearable, like going through the shock a second and third time.

When will I ever feel safe enough to sleep again? I need to stay awake. I go to my study, searching for wisdom. Books are a comfort, but I need the dynamic of immediacy. Yes, the Internet. Good idea. I log on and key the words "women," "bereavement," and "grief." I cannot bring myself to type "widow." It is not yet part of my vocabulary. I am a woman who has lost her partner. This is more than enough to bear.

Willowgreen Press comes up, and I click on pages of writing so like my own; I am struck by the synchronicity of it. Similar forces that fostered my own point of view have nurtured this author. Unlike the books I've been offered by well-meaning friends, I can take this in: this treatise on grief, written by someone I respect. Respect. I see the word in a new way now, as in "to view again." Is wisdom a state where we are reminded of things we already know? I send a note to Willowgreen.

March 12

As God creates with chaos, we respond with ritual.

The mass comforts me; my loss overwhelms me; the mourners flood me with tears and wash me clean. They blow life into my own collapsing lungs with their grief, love, and stories. As this happens, I am buoyed for a spell. It seems this is a time that when you dig deeply enough, everything is shared.

I am surrounded by so many people, the way cotton gauze may pack and protect a wound. The contrast between the public outpouring and the need to contain my very private pain seems surreal.

My challenge is to remain steady, even as I feel an overwhelming urge to let go. As if crossing a suspension bridge, I use my intention as a walking stick, a balancing beam, to hold steady. I'm experienced enough to know when it doesn't matter if I give in—when it won't be self-limiting—in order to feel some relief.

Up against all the abstraction—where do they go, what happens to those who have passed away?—we need to find a beautiful and tranquil place where we lay our loved ones to rest. My conscious decision to take care of myself guides me to find the perfect spot where I can visit him. His children and I spend the better part of the day seeking *his* place.

How we perceive is how we proceed. And I must create the new perceptions—the new mindsets—that will carry me forward:

- Coping/pragmatic
- Psychological
- Philosophical
- Spiritual
- Artistic
- Learning

Where do I begin...????

March 13

Fatigue is my enemy. I shall not indulge my fears. When I'm not tired, it's easier to be strong. When I'm overtaken with fatigue, a world made of all my illusions begins to tumble in on me. I am more and more alone. Melting into disappearance, me...

Alone, I have come to realize how healing a simple presence can be, and I regret the times I felt that my presence would be non-significant in anyone's grief. I've been reading the teachings of Buddha, reciting the Jesus prayer, reciting the schma. (a simple declaration of "faith" in the Jewish tradition.) I can't get enough of rituals, even borrowed rituals. I am building my rituals of comfort. One step at a time. One day at a time. I need the structure that each and all of these provide.

March 14, 1999

Willowgreen has sent a reply. I can't believe I received a response! A real person, a former clergyman turned writer and publisher. Our exchange begins...

Dear Dr. Jim Miller, I had first written to him. "On March 9, 1999, I suddenly became a widow. The unexpected loss of my husband propelled me into a new reality…one most of us don't want to imagine." As a psychologist who had (for over 20 years) specialized in the process of change and transition, I searched for sources of support. I found myself wandering the resources of the Internet. I used a search engine to make my reality tangible and typed in 'bereavement-coping.'

"I chose your pages and was gratified to find that your writing and sensibilities were in complete concordance with the focus of my life's work and now my own personal journey. I found your tone and suggestions soothing; almost identical to my own writing. I would love to correspond further and if I can contribute in any way to your beautiful site, I would be happy to do so."

Hello, Andrea, he has replied. "It's good to hear from you. March 9 is so recent. How did your husband die? Do you have good support? I can understand how you would feel our writing has some of the same flavor. It came through in your e-mail. Let's stay in touch."

And we did. Strangers in a strange land, we continued to correspond. Our correspondence continues still. We never know from what direction we may be lifted and supported.

March 15

The tiny familiar actions of life create the deepest despair. I do the wash and feel such an unbearable sadness. As I lean weakly against the washing machine, overcome, my mind engages in irrational, irrelevant debate…

> Despair: *How can his clothes be here when he is not?*
> Uncertainty: *Should I wash them?*
> Outrage: *Why should I?*
> Control: *Why shouldn't I? I can wash these things if I want.*
> Rationality: *What am I thinking???*

A sudden clutching pain in my midsection overwhelms me. I feel the rising of tears in my throat and behind my eyes. His presence and his absence, both at once! Such a weird paradox of existence. I grab his unwashed t-shirt and hold it close. Upstairs, I place it under my pillow. I take comfort where I find it.

March 17

My son has been with me, seeing me through the worst of times. Even with him here, I've been sleeping in my clothes, feeling too vulnerable to sleep in nightwear. What if someone comes unexpectedly to visit? Because that seems to be what is happening. My life is open to the public in so far as our communities have a strong need to reach out and share the grieving process. Simultaneously, my instincts are private. I need protection, even from those who would protect me. I need to be guarded. Soon I'll be sleeping completely alone…again. No visiting relatives or friends. Alone. Again.

I ache all the time, in every spare minute, terrified that I'll never get over this loss.

I cry periodically, sick at the thought of my grown-up child returning to his own life and leaving me here in this unfamiliarity. This lack of family—this unusual singularity—I am nauseated by the fragility of life, the fragility of connections. How quickly, how irrevocably, we can lose the ones we love. How empty life is without them.

One day my husband was with me, wholehearted and loving. In an instant, he was completely gone from me, without a final formal goodbye. Life is forever changed, and I'm on a journey into what is "next." At times, an inexplicable rush of exhilaration overtakes me, like turbulence at 30,000 feet. Then I'm dropped heartlessly into the void, lonely again, and ridden with anxiety.

I am aware of how important acknowledgment can become. Validating his life feels necessary to me, like breathing in. Sustenance. A balance of life as it existed against the death that is real now. Appreciating the recognition of his life through the eyes of his community is a bonus I would never have imagined could make such a difference in my own ability to accept this loss.

My hold on reality is so tenuous that I write down what I see because what I see is the only reality I can accept. What I can observe—this inventory of sensation—functions as a handrail keeping me upright, and it is all I can trust right now.

Much as I do during my mindfulness meditations, when I note what is, I create an inventory to remind myself that although the "we" is no longer, he is the one who is dead. I am alive:

- I am surprised that I can receive the condolences of so many people and keep my heart open.

- I am blessed with love and support all around me.

- I am flooded with food and flowers.

- I am afraid of drowning in my sorrow.

- I am deeply aware that this event signifies an incredible turning point in my life.

- ᴥ I am awed by the power of life and death to bypass my own small arrogance.

- ᴥ I am being tested.

- ᴥ I don't know what to expect.

- ᴥ I must remember to breathe.

- ᴥ I am incredibly strong…when I shut down feelings, I can move more easily.

- ᴥ I am in suspended animation between two worlds.

I have not allowed myself to fully express my rage and pain. I am afraid that, when I do, I will be either irretrievable or inconsolable and will wander, forever lost in self-pity. I hope I can rely on my ability to resist dwelling in the past.

Life is already changing. I am waking earlier, greeting the dawn, and trying to live in each present moment rather than in the future. The only safe, certain place is "now." I take comfort in this modicum of control.

March 17

A week has passed. I stare at the calendar. A week already? How can it be?

When I'm feeling calm and in control, I get afraid that the fear and pain will ambush me. I weep whenever I return home from time away. My brave façade and sense of hope are in sharp contrast with the emptiness of my reality. Such self-regulation is exhausting. I fall into a choppy sleep. When I awaken, I reach for my journal and begin to write…

"On Having One's Life Pass in Front of One's Eyes Unsolicited"

One day you have your life
Such as it is
The requirements of
Living
And the
Routines
Of existence
Habits
As they are
They get us through
Deadened or alive
And one day
That life is shattered
In one last gasp
Silent
At a desk
On a Tuesday morning
As ordinary as the one before
Except
Turning points come

Unannounced
And cold March mornings
With automatic
Farewells
And the usual
Business
Stretching out
A path to walk
As usual
A cold and sunny morning
Just another in a long line
Of endless conversations
About other people's lives
Little did I know
That for weeks to come
I would be
The center of
This conversation.
All touch
And talk
Directed
At the core
Of my raw and
Deepening wound
My bleeding heart
Swabbed
Endlessly
The rough tongues
Of a thousand cats
Licking and licking

Until
Care hurts more
Than pain itself.
No beat skipped
An endless procession
The protection
Of mourners
Crying in my arms
And depositing their totems
Their tokens
Sacred offerings
Their aching
Reminders
Of the tall and
Charming
Lionhearted man
Graced with our enviable love.
And once the
Stream of mourners—
The human testament of
Witnesses for
His life
Taper to a trickle
There shines
The pilgrimage—
My own sweet
Soldiers of
Support.
From the darkest
Corners of my

At Ground Zero: Words While Walking Wounded

Past and present
They emerge laying
Familiar
Memories at my feet
Love and inspirations
Bread and fruit
Thread themselves
Through my private
Suffering and story
Shared compassion
Tiny buoyant
Points of light
Years of
Journey
Backlit
With entreaties
Inducements
And endorsements—
Prayers
For me to carry on.
Unsolicited
Cheerleaders
On the road to
Inevitable despair
To loss
To death
To nothingness—
We are all a
Winding band of
Valiant

Vagabonds—
Lost and generous
Souls and siblings
Willing to share
Illusions
Simply to survive.

Dear Reader: As you must know by now, I rely upon my journal entries and poems to create a safe distance—a reality I can accept—when I find myself in the midst of chaos. These creative outpourings anchor me and remind me that my essential identity, though shaken, is still vibrant and strong.

By sharing with you like this, I hope to show you how valuable it can be to develop a daily habit of expressing yourself in ways that feed your soul. For you, it may not be words. Your method of choice may be dance, or drawing, or painting, or music. It could be hiking or swimming or some type of craft. You may find comfort working with clay, or wood; gardening may bring you in touch with the very essence of life itself. Just telling your story, even over again, to friends, to whoever asks, can be your method of finding your way.

I urge you to embrace whatever it is that works for you—whatever allows you the space to seek and be yourself. At times, it may seem that it is all you have.

Chapter 2

Aftershock Overload:
The Wildly Shifting Pendulum

*Just breathe… You're okay in
this moment, and you'll be okay.*

*Those first weeks following the end of my life as I knew it are
filled with a kind of back and forth motion. I desire to hold
onto the preciousness of that sacred relationship. I vacillate
between tolerating and not being able to tolerate the pain
of its ending.*

This pain is also the stinging pain of confrontation with existential truth, with the pain of having and then not having safety, security; with having and then not having tools to cope with each new challenge that comes. I fantasize about fast-forwarding out of the agony of this place and into an unknown, but less turbulent, future.

A certain receptivity can accompany desperation: a willingness to push beyond the ordinary and habitual. I knew I could not simply rely on how I might have behaved BHD—Before His Death. Rather, I had to stay close to my own impulses and intuitions, knowing they were the inner song of my survival.

Despite this (because of it?), my own healing journey is progressing. I am proud of my ability to reach in deeply, to keep my heart open, to write and work and perform under conditions of extreme emotionality without depersonalizing or disassociating (too much.)

The writing process can be perfectionistic for me, and I'm surprised at how this extrovert is content to sit for long periods at the computer, not seeing another soul while spending hours doing methodical paperwork, estate work, and so on. Despite everything, in those moments when the pain recedes, I feel a sense of peace and pride.

March 17

I am back at work. My office is the same, and I am different. My clients are different too. They seem to watch my every move. Some of them seem reluctant to see me. They don't know what to expect. They worry their problems will seem silly or small by comparison. They think, "How can I ask her to listen to my petty concerns?" Fortunately, they call and make appointments anyway. And they're met with my broken shining heart, fully exposed. Very intimate, very meaningful on many levels.

Magically, I feel as if I am in a state of grace. I love each one of them exponentially and feel my heart and arms expanding to include *all* pain. There is nothing localized about my compassion. My broken heart includes theirs, and my work matters to me now more than ever before. Peaceful surrender to every movement and moment of aliveness informs my days.

I am deeply grateful I can work during this tragic and vulnerable time. Something inexpressibly open and available in me touches each person in my circle of clients and friends. Somehow, this deep pain has a kind of force field around it—can it be, in some odd way, protective? I wonder. Does tragedy excuse me from incurring additional hurt? Does grief cover the waterfront on some level, all suffering being the essence of being human? I think it does.

March 18

Although not even two weeks have passed, I have taken the first steps toward change and transition, consciously and unconsciously attempting to put distance between my life with my husband and my current circumstance. I know that I must do this to make some kind of sense of my days. I'm carrying the absurd immediacy of his life within my own, as if we're still together, only to awaken to the lie that this is. The drop of my stomach from illusion to reality is so steep and dizzying. So I pretend I'm in a time tunnel hurtling forward into space. Forward feels better than backward. Reducing life to movement feels necessary. And I'm grateful that springtime promises renewal and hope.

Yet, even as I move forward, distancing myself from all that I knew, I find myself reaching out to the gentle clergyman at Willowgreen Press, needing to anchor some essential part of myself to all that I had.

Dear Jim Miller, I write:

"Your reply to my e-mail brought a burst of joyful tears. It's amazing to reach into cyberspace, out of the haunting sorrow of sudden loss, and be met with such interest and kindness. In response to your questions... My husband was an extraordinary man. A fifty-three-year-old educator with over thirty years of service to a prestigious school district as an elementary school principal, his contribution was large, and the mourning community is immense. The children presently enrolled, and many years' worth of parents and students now growing and grown, have created an outpouring of daunting proportion.

Ours was a rich, mature relationship on so many levels. We had met after each of us had experienced years of being single, following our divorces. We had worked together, resolving staff-development issues for his school, and then went on to have a wonderful, conscious, and evolving relationship that lasted for thirteen years. I had sought someone who would be my anchor, my sanctuary, and I found these qualities in him.

Although I have begun to see a few clients each day, managing my new reality is more than a full-time job. I cannot tell you how much I cherish my practice, now more than ever. It is a bright jewel in the stormy sea, and my own years of service to others have created an entirely separate outpouring of grief and support from those whose lives I've touched. Many of them feel they knew my husband through knowing me and how I am.

This is a huge life-changing event whose implications can only be barely intuited at this time. What I do know is that I am surrounded by countless blessings in the form of love of every kind…from strangers, from those in our pasts resurfacing now, from people I hardly know from his educational life, and from my parents (a double blessing) and our grown-up children (although they all live far away). And then, when I viewed your website, your insights and your writing offered even more support. I am truly blessed."

Hello, Andrea, he replies.

"Your husband sounds like such a vital man. I can't imagine what it would be like to lose my wife after finding such happiness with her. Blessings as you continue through these days and acclimate yourself to your loss. With those others who hold you close, I will too."

Moments of calm are shattered by moments of panic. In the middle of the night, I awaken to find that my son, 22, is out visiting with friends and has not yet arrived home. It's 4:00 a.m., and I start to panic. I call him and learn that he's still with friends he had met for a late dinner and socializing. I'm worried that he still has to drive home, but his voice sounds clear and confident.

This is more than a mother's concern. At this point, life in general feels too fragile to trust. I get scared about the unknown and insecure about the future. This week feels as short as a day and as long as a year—all at the same time. The quiet is too vast for me, and I lose myself in it. I must stay centered and connected. Being alone doesn't feel like an option I would want to choose.

March 19

I have a wonderful dinner with family, only to return home demoralized. I'm plummeting tonight, trying to stay sane, probably exhausted, feeling lonely and depleted. Dismal.

"Just breathe," I tell myself. *"You're okay in this moment, and you'll be okay."*

March 20

In the midst of gathering the tattered remnants of my life and returning to work, I am confronted with new expenses that have emerged from the rubble and now demand my attention. Responsible Executrix is a part of the new identity I am forced to assume. Once loved, held safe, and validated as part of a couple, I am stripped of my protections. Tasks that we (I) fully expected to share now fall on me alone. In the midst of mental and emotional confusion, how will I sort them out? How will I learn the habits of such detailed administration when this kind of accounting and accountability has never been my strength?

Grief and frustration, helplessness and despair, threaten to sink me. The only defense is to keep on keeping on. To separate my feelings of being lost from those of feeling overwhelmed, I must embrace my ability to be resourceful. I must choose survival; I must cultivate determination and hope. I must agree to learn beyond my limits. All bets are off on anything that keeps me small.

March 21

The symbols of my husband's ordinary life, such as his wallet—its contents, its credit cards, and its identification cards—haunt me. Who is he? Who was he? Where is he now?

The Buddhists talk about the "bardo" as a waiting area of forty days' duration before the spirit goes on to the next place. I attempt to imagine where my husband's spirit might be and how he might see me from that distant place, trying to cope, trying to make sense of his life, of our life and now mine. If I give away his clothes, am I giving away more than I'm willing to part with? If I keep his clothes in the closet, what kind of lie am I living?

Tiny decisions feel monumental.

Removing his traces feels like an erasure of his life, like a betrayal of our marital bond.

Keeping his clothes in the closet is both comforting and taunting. I am not good at endorsing him through his possessions, nor am I yet sturdy enough to adopt a heartless purging of his symbolic self. What to do?

By imagining him, I keep myself in a relationship with him. This affords me a strange comfort. Sometimes I ask him directly what he'd want me to do. I write letters to him, appealing to his wisdom. Surely I know him well enough to imagine his response.

I think back. We didn't really say good-bye. He, all dressed and ready to go to work, called out his usual *"See you later."* Moments later, I noticed the cat on my bedroom window ledge register the movement of Richard's car as it left. I sensed his departure and our strong connection but had no idea how radical a departure it would turn out to be.

I recall now a widowed client of mine who felt a similar kind of betrayal. She actually moved out of her bedroom and closed its door, sleeping on a recliner in the living room because she didn't have the stomach to face the rupture of their connection by sorting through familiar possessions and getting rid of them. She felt tortured and stuck by the specter of dispensing with *things* as a parallel of dispensing with *him*.

Pre-warned by our therapeutic relationship, I didn't want to let myself in for the torture of facing this. I find a way to satisfy this ambivalence. I decide to call a friend to see if he can make good use of my husband's wardrobe. My inner sensibility is satisfied with this solution. I need to create the space to heal; to be courageous in the face of the emptiness. And to satisfy myself that this upwardly striving education professional will take the chosen items to a level of high achievement and esteem. This decision, at least, is one I can live with. If his outer identity can go on to new heights, I can let go.

However abstract, my heart is quiet and resolved. The empty closet can symbolize a place for hope, for something else to grow. Like a fertile field or a planter with fresh earth. I choose to believe that emptiness carries a quality that invites transformation.

Interesting how we have choices about what to believe. Recognizing that we have choice. Recognizing that in choosing our beliefs, we raise the spinnaker on our own little sailboat just enough to balance the wind that threatens to capsize us.

March 23

The hopelessness of discouraging times seems endless. It helps me not at all to know that this is because the mind tends to play with the hurtful, just as a young child plays with a loose tooth all night long. When my reservoir of usable soul refreshment is at drought levels, I resort to other people's formulations about life. The quickest injections of life-enhancing thoughts are found on audio CDs. I wear headphones to drown out the sound of my own anxious obsessions.

Even if I don't hear every word, the experience of someone else's message provides me with a thought form and sound vibration that changes my emotional state. I keep a shelf stocked and visit it often in my most trying times.

March 24

Like a fine rain, I'm bathed in grief until I begin to move through my day, vibrating with others in my sacred contract as confidant or coach. Such vibration turns the sadness into mist, and the vaporous cloud is burned off by the strong love light of friendship... like the rays of the sun, reaching me, keeping me exposed, relating in real time.

In role-model mode, I reinforce my strength and my ability to be with people, with clients. I know I can embody inspiration if I keep moving. When I keep moving, the sadness doesn't accumulate, nor does it cling to every fiber of my body and threaten to drown me.

March 25

The self-protective part of me—the part that wants to hide or disappear—and the part that cannot turn away from life and its responsibilities is engaged in a constant dialogue.

Making the switch from privacy to social involvement creates a high level of anxiety. Once I'm comfortable, I don't want to change. Facing aloneness after a day with people can feel threatening and unbearably lonely. Conversely, moving out of the cave of dark despair into a day of contact-intensive participation can produce a parallel wave of uneasiness. After a while, I find a rhythm. I use this time between two worlds to better understand the role of transition on a larger level, telling myself that this suffering must be worth the lessons we learn from it.

The most exciting work I do is with folks who begin to feel the glimmer of a shift in their life direction and who find themselves ready to honor the promptings wherever they may lead. My own tragedy has left me with vast spaces to reconfigure, and I am the type to jump ahead to follow my visions, although my body might not be as ready as my mind to embrace the shift. So, a particular challenge is to keep myself—body and mind—integrated. And this involves feeling more pain. But it's not a solid wall of pain, and if I keep breathing, I can move the clouds and let the light through.

March 27

This morning, I am driving with my son to visit a dear friend. The idea is to have a reunion and to surround myself with the closest possible net of love and support that I can pull tightly around me. I've brought my cat on the journey, unwilling to leave any essential part of "me"—any being I love—behind.

As we drink our coffee, I watch my cat adjust to new surroundings. It is a house full of animals: two golden retrievers, a coddled Himalayan, and a street cat. My cat's tail uncharacteristically low to the ground, he moves in slow motion, cautiously testing each step as he searches for his place of best view, smartest defense, widest perspective. His brown nose twitches, his white whiskers tremulous as he ventures out of his carrier a little at a time.

From the sanctuary of my friend's familiar space, I am aware that I have been venturing out of my own comfort zone in much the same way.

March 29

These weeks following the death of my life as I knew it are filled with a kind of back and forth motion. I feel a desire to hold onto the preciousness of sacred relationships, a vacillation between tolerating and not being able to tolerate the pain of ending, the pain of truth, the pain of losing the trusted mirror of one's soul through marriage, and the desire to fast forward out of the agony into some unknown but less turbulent promise of a future.

April 1

I find it imperative to put solid new experiences between today and the destructive episode of loss. Understanding the workings of the mind, I know that new, fully dimensional experiences will begin to accumulate mass between my life as it was and my life as it is now. This observation forces me to address the mandate to build my new reality, to stock it with new memories, to get a life.

What *is* a life, anyhow?

I am obsessed with the issue of personal meaning, of significance versus insignificance.

Where do I focus my energies?

Inspired, I know what I must do: I must go everywhere I may be inclined. Say yes to travel and to conferences and to creative learning experiences and to time with new friends and new places. I must convert the energy of meaningful newness into a way of packing my widening wound with insulation from stinging loss. I must stock my mental library with rich volumes that do not drag me backwards but rather that urge me forward, evolving and expanding beyond the lingering, soul-destroying pain.

April 2

I've overslept.

Choosing one of Richard's sweatshirts, I roll up the sleeves and begin the first of several episodes of sorting and disposing. These are the first tentative movements towards making space and gaining perspective. As I do this, small treasures trigger remembered responses, and I am driven to confront my memories as the insubstantial present fades...

I find a snapshot of the country house shared within our extended families. I recall the many times, on those weekends that we called it home away from home, that I drove there alone. How often his work kept him in the city, so tired, so late. I remember how, during so many of those lonely times, I yearned to have him with me. Other times, though, how glad I was of the solitude; of the time to gather my energies and explore my thoughts alone. I feel overwhelmed by guilt and despair as I remember my conflicting emotions...

Why isn't he here?

How could he leave me alone so often?

And then, embracing the peace and tranquility...

What time will he get here?

How much time do I have to cherish this, alone?

I gaze into the photograph and imagine his spirit in the house. The fragrance, the wood, and the rooms we shared. Tears begin to fill my eyes, blurring the image.

Stop it!

Talking to myself and to him, I bargain with myself:

Maybe I was more here, without you, on balance, than with you?

Yes, darling, I was here without you, before you. And here I am again. Alone. Again.

If life is a tapestry, what do we do when precious stitches are suddenly dropped? Is it possible to reweave a life? To mend this gaping hole?

So many times, I wanted to be alone. I remember once after a long, dark ride on a rainy Friday night, I was squirming away from having to relate to anyone. I recall that it was my idea that we pretend we were alone. I suggested that we not speak and that we write on sticky notes:

Where did you put the cookies?

Did you bring the extension cord?

I wanted so much at times to have my own space and to be relieved of the burdens of close living. And now I have it. Riptide.

April 3

Now I ache to do the opposite of that.

Alone in reality, but with you in every way on a spiritual level, I can still communicate with you. I can share my truth with you.

I am trying not to cry. Gritting my teeth, I can't allow the feelings to overwhelm me. I am undone, and yet there are moments of surprising equanimity in this period too, as if I've always been alone. And as if I never allowed myself to fully attach.

The truth is that, despite our years together, being a couple still felt like a novelty, one that I was just learning to accept.

I have come to believe that staying aware of impermanence is prudent; being aware that loving attachment on the material plane is a temporary joy. Knowing this affirms the intensity of love. (Note to self: This advice would be helpful in a book I will write in the future called " *A Bride's Guide to Widowhood.*" I must remember this!)

April 6

I break down in the supermarket. This complacent normalcy—all these people whose worlds have *not* been violated—is an affront to me. A very simple and ordinary errand has now become overwhelming. The void is too prevalent. I flee to save my sanity, empty shopping bag in hand.

April 7

Today I have returned to the country house. It's bearable, though sadness lurks in its corners. I keep a discipline about not indulging it. A person can be in control, as a protective measure. A person can take only so much. One can engage one's will to avoid unnecessary pain. One has choice.

Wasn't it just the Sunday before you died that I held you in gratitude and with tears streaming hotly, hidden in your embrace, crying in your arms about being afraid to depend on you? You reassured me that you'd always be there for me, but I wouldn't let myself melt into the seductive security of that.

What if you were taken from me?

What if one of us were to leave?

And then you did.

Dear Reader: This time of shifting moods can be frightening—both for you and your loved ones. As you've seen from my journal entries, the emotional pendulum left me restless and uncertain, made it impossible for me to stay still. Physically moving from place to place gave me a welcome opportunity to use my energy in productive, albeit exhausting, ways.

What is most common in our times of grief is the desire to reach into the abstract to make sense of a concrete loss. Seeking comfort from astrological readings, having Tarot cards read, consulting psychics or mediums whose predictions hold the promise of contact from "beyond the veil"... How little it takes to quiet our hearts.

It is important to accept that this very human process—as we strive to internalize those aspects we hold most dear—takes as long as it takes. And that for each of us, this period of time is unique; it cannot be defined or hastened; it must be allowed to unfold in its own special way.

Another stress that you will be forced to address—no matter how well you may have planned—is the financial responsibility that you now carry alone. It is very likely that this will happen to you too—at a time when you are least equipped to deal with it—and I urge you to find someone you can trust to help you make sense of it all.

In the midst of your grief, barely coping, you may also find that people still depend on you as they have always done, turning to you for your strength, although they should know you are feeling vulnerable, lost, and alone. Ironically, it is this focus, this positive energy required of you, that will help you burn off the fog of disorientation and move forward.

The price you pay—in switching back and forth from privacy to social involvement—can create moments of anxiety and reluctance. Take comfort in the knowledge that you *will* find your rhythm. You *will* learn to embrace the transition and welcome each new day. Each back and forth—each introversion and extroversion—contains its own aspects of release and relief.

In the face of such indelible loss, it is easy to feel that your life began and ended with the loved one who is gone. The truth that you will come to learn— as I came to learn about myself, once I found the strength—is that the time you shared was not the sum total of your existence. What it was, instead, was a treasured, precious interlude.

I share these details to help you; to urge you to listen to your heart and ignore those who might presume that you don't have a right to the feelings that now engulf you. No matter where or when you may have met your loved one, no matter what roads you traveled, you have earned this time to celebrate the love you shared and to mourn its passing.

Chapter 3

Deconstruction:
Sorting through the Rubble

This is a time of tremendous grace,
tremendous pain,
and tremendous recognition.
Please grant me the equanimity to use
the time wisely and to grow from within.

Coming to terms with this new identity—this single me—
is a journey along a divided highway. On the one hand,

I am newly born, uncertain of my steps, a stranger in a strange land. At the same time, it is as if I am a wanderer returning, revisiting my past.

Though I am a Virgin Widow, innocent in the face of my husband's sudden death, I am not a child. This was my second marriage, not my first, and in this coupling, I was not a Virgin Bride.

And so it was natural that part of my journey of remembrance takes me back to those other lives to escape the pain.

Bittersweet memories are waiting in my jewelry box, where I find the keepsakes that return me to young womanhood. As I gently open each compartment, I glimpse the woman I was before I knew this man I mourn. Instead of looking in the mirror, I look to the past. I stop a while and pay tribute. I recapture the true essence of myself and learn who I must be from those I loved and those who loved me.

In my practice, I see this often: Clients who face grim realities choose to postpone the inevitable. Now, as if at a distance, I watch as I indulge in a similar escape. Does this diminish the grief? Does it minimize the despair? Not at all: No matter how far you run, it is always there. And if we are to learn and grow and change with dignity and grace, this we must understand and embrace: In our lifetimes, we are many things to many people—to our mothers and fathers, sisters and brothers, lovers, husbands, children, and friends—and each of these many roles shapes the people we are today. Married once, twice, or many times does not change the love we feel and the grief we endure. Who we are is a product of who we were.

April 8

I spend a day with my sister in Northampton. I feel compelled to cover all the territory I can, confronting as many memories as possible. On the one hand, I feel sickened by my loss, by encountering all the places we visited together. At the same time, there's the gentle residue of pleasant, sweet memories. I force myself to visit and make new memories here. There is a challenge to move past the memorializing. Leaving flowers, a piece of jewelry, or a shell as a marker, I make the conscious decision that these are "me" places now, places I am reclaiming. Having sought and found closure, I will be able to go to these places without fear of tripping over the past.

At this point, I am still numbed by the onslaughts of sorrow. I scrupulously push away the quiet, transient moments of self-pity. Confronting the past and acknowledging the future, I make small gestures that buy normalcy: a new comforter for my bedroom, some gifts for close friends. At the very moment that I have become a widow, two of my best friends are marrying this summer: two weddings and a funeral, I think wryly. It is bittersweet, yet it still affirms the promise that life goes on.

We arrive back home and I write out one hundred and twenty twenty-four "thank you for your kind expression of sympathy" cards. The ritual is deadening.. I am re-frozen in the ice clamp of grief.

April 9

At a lovely brunch with neighbors, one month to the day, I am present only in body, smiling and nodding, going through the motions. Meanwhile, I am caught up in memory, replaying the morning he died. Amidst the swirl of chatter and mealtime clatter, I am far away, engaged in a spirited inner-monologue debate:

The very fact that there was nothing extraordinary about that morning is offensive. Really, if there had been a crisis of some kind…something…anything…I would have been aware, engaged in the battle, but there was nothing to prepare for, no possibility of preparation.

How could he die? He was so monitored, so checked, so healthy. How dare he?

My eyes glaze over with giant tears that magnify the words on this page. How arrogant to think we can "prevent" or "manage" death.

I listen to Judy Collins....*too far in my past to have memories of him in this music. That's why I choose it.* Life moves on. Focus. Stay in the present. Stay with what is; relax into the feelings. They are what they are. Only waves of sensation...they curl, they intensify, they crest, and they dissipate. Breathe...follow the breath, rising and falling...ever-changing...nothing is permanent...not pleasure...not pain.

April 10

It's hard to say what depresses my mood. Mostly night, I suppose, with the darkening hours, the onset of fatigue, watching a movie with a human theme, catching a riff of music. I try not to listen to music that might trigger memories or melancholy. I'm alert for the stalking and empty black hole of hopelessness that, so far, has not ambushed me tonight. At least, not yet...

It still seems like yesterday that he died...such a relentlessly long yesterday. In this new life, there's only Yesterday, when he died, and Today. All of my life seems incredible, unreal by contrast. Am I really living suspended, waiting for an "until" of sorts?

"Until" I get used to it?

"Until" life changes?

"Until" I get rescued?

"Until" the next inevitable life-changing event?

Fiction and nonfiction, these days. I am writing to keep myself sane. I am oozing poetry to capture and contain a panoply of emotions: At times, my mind fools me into hardly remembering him. At other times, I know I will never forget. He will never return. The question that haunts me is, *"How will I make sense of his life within mine as I move forward in time without him?"*

I need courage. I need to practice courage to face the scary feelings during the day. When fatigued or worn down, I go into the dark spiral, charcoal gray, surrendering. Having taken the advice of my doctors (reluctantly), I look forward to my ¼ Xanax to help me escape from the pain into sleep, where the darkness can't reach me.

April 11

Counting my blessings is like counting sheep. I have the means to travel, and I'm taking full advantage. I need to place distance between the before and after of my separate lives. I need time to breathe without watching the clock. The promise of a new nomadic existence, the experiment of leaving home is a consolation prize. I count the days. A week seems like an eternity.

April 12

Chanting pleasantries as one would reassure a child that everything will be all right, I feel obsessed with just existing. Hearing myself say pleasant things is reassuring, the auditory as a hedge against being overtaken with useless obsession. I feel a self-righteous entitlement to disconnect from "the now." I am just getting through this time the best I can. Doing what I can to take care of myself; to unplug and distract. I am building new patterns, performing basic physical upkeep, honoring and acknowledging my community of fellow mourners, continuing the work of the estate settlement, and maintaining my responsibility to clients. And it is almost more than I can bear.

I try to keep faith about love in my life—all forms of it, the certainty of it, the expression of it, the necessity of it. Even as I weep, I know that I am still alive. This living with the deadness of my husband has a way of contaminating my psyche, as if a part of me is actually dead. Each time I separate from this phenomenon and realize my true and actual aliveness, I feel surprised and relieved. At a curiously detached level, this is interesting to me.

April 13

The absolute lifeline of writing helps manage my moments of greatest sorrow and despair. Even when the expression is repetitive and self-serving, it is antiseptic. The action of pouring words onto a page is like applying gauze to an unhealed wound, protecting and framing what is ravaged and broken, sopping up the blood.

Mercifully for others, my writing practice absorbs much of the seemingly inexhaustible stream of internal conversation that plagues the grieving person. And the movement of my hand on the page or my fingers on the keys allows for a kinetic and percussive outlet of emotions—a way of permitting its flow in a continual and necessary rhythm of release.

April 16

A childhood friend is here, helping me tackle the home office: the epicenter of his remaining physical presence. She is crying as she clears the shelves. Knowing that I need her relentless approach, she is assertive, demanding that I remove everything.

"But this…but that…"

I wistfully finger little artifacts and items that feel like precious pieces of his life. She's right, nevertheless. Sentimentality is too much for either of us to bear. My energy is drained each time I enter this room. And I must use this room as the center of the estate settlement operation so that *my* work space remains a sanctuary for those who come to visit me.

Again, I force myself to let go of the notion of keeping him in my heart through his things. I choose carefully, placing a few mementos in a treasure chest to be opened, if necessary, later on in life…down the road, when the emotional landscape has changed.

"There, there," I murmur to myself. "It won't always be like this."

April 17

I move on to the next frontier: the bedroom. His clothing holds both maudlin comfort and unnecessary temptations to fall—free fall—into the abyss of missing. It will be better to come home to a bedroom I can call my own. Empty as it might feel, it will give me a better chance to start clean in a new phase. I push through this difficulty with pure will, and as I do, I feel the energy shift from sacred storage to sacred spaciousness to allow for "the next." I'm surprised that the emptiness feels like potential more than it torments me with absence.

I feel a growing need to create a physical transition in time and space. Increasingly, it is not enough to clear a room. As my thoughts turn to Arizona, where the perpetual sunny weather promises no real challenges, I move to make it happen.

Charged with energy at my last-minute decision, I pack. My thoughts revolve around the days ahead. My son is there, and I have friends. In a lighter, brighter atmosphere, I will have respite.

April 20

Last morning before departure. Difficult to think about leaving Java, my cat. Still, the smallest separation from anything I love feels threatening. Yesterday was a disaster; I kept losing it. Packing was overwhelming. On the verge of tears all evening, I was unfocused. Finally, I stuff too much into a suitcase that will be impossible to carry, wishing I could fit myself into a tiny carry on bag—it would be more efficient. I feel groundless.

Later on... I need to write truthfully of my numbness, my despair, my nausea. Living within the change, trying to stay steady and not look back, not projecting into the future. To not hope; to not grasp. To stay as clear and as present as possible. The past few days have been impossibly dizzying and demanding: lists upon lists of unfinished business. Leaving unfinished business is so daunting. The practice; the phone calls; the house; the estate settlement process; even the cat and his needs. When I'm so frenzied, I lose optimism; I lose my finely calculated control. So, vulnerability turns to negativity. Even tonight, at dinner with family, I scan the dining room and am somehow reminded of my absent mate. The pain is so unbearable that I hide from it, pretending to myself that I haven't thought of him. Skimming and skating the surface of my mind, fleeing my memories and sensory experiences, trying to go dead inside. Quiet, still, stealthy, sneaking around the aroused feelings, trying to escape unnoticed and unnoticing, and every night I get into bed with my heart thumping.

April 21

I take flight. A long, choppy plane ride—five hours—but I'm too tired to care. I'm quiet. Hardly speaking; hardly thinking. Simply being is such an accomplishment. I look for room to breathe under the high, cloudless sky of Sedona.

Ever since my first visit to the West—when I was in my 20s—I realized a special connection with the spaciousness. The air seemed magically clean, the sky so big I felt free. By comparison, though the East is my home, it has always made me feel compressed, somehow, confined. Here in Arizona once again, I find it easier to think, to feel, to be. I feel a suspension of my old identity. It's such a relief.

April 25

I am "un-Richarding" my associations and experiences and dreams. An "un-process" of letting go; emptying a phase of life.

I scamper among the red rocks and grasses to find a perfect rock on which to sit. It juts out from the side of the hill, in the shade. No humans are immediately around me. It offers a perfect panoramic view.

A flash of last night, when a friend of a friend made it clear that he might want to get to know me better: a married man, fairly trustworthy, yet a male animal nonetheless, perfectly polite and yet still a vibe. *And I, feeling fragile and vulnerable, like a virgin: a Virgin Widow.*

Escaping these thoughts, I take out pen and paper and begin to write…

Pine quiet
Red rock
Birdsong and tears
Awed by immensity
Beckoned back in years
Times of love and dreaming
Gently set in stone
Smelling of eternity
Mine now to re-own

April 26

My family heads to Utah, trying their best to cajole me into coming along. But I crave solitude. At last, I am ready to sleep alone, to be left to breathe, to think my thoughts.

I have longed to be alone here in the clear air with the pines and junipers and my own sense of myself and how things are. The unsettling aspect of choosing to be alone is the possibility of uncontained sorrow and unchecked emotion, which are scary in their infinity. There's always the fear that I'll never come out of such feelings; that I'll drown in them. And yet if I'm carefully observant, my actual experience will be one of a natural self-limiting event. The paroxysms of suffering will find a way of subsiding on their own. Like a sea, its power will dissipate in white caps.

A friend offers to take me by motorcycle into the wilderness of Soldier's Pass. This would have been the site of our dream home. This becomes one of those times of sudden, over-brimming grief and sorrow and self-pity, the tears beginning to leak out as I stride across the ledges to the Seven Sacred Pools. I barely make it to a red rocky overhang that promises shade before my grief spills uncontrollably from being under such tight reins, such tight restraint.

Pulling myself above the little path, I collapse under a pinion. Encircled by red rocks and sweet grass, I curl into a fetal position and let the sobbing—deep and rolling—begin. Endlessly falling and sliding into the thrashing current of despair, I cry till my eyes feel as if they're hanging out of my sockets and my guts begin to wrench. As the wind blows up, I writhe on the ground, calling pathetically to my husband. He does not answer.

When I lie back to breathe, I look to the sky and am startled to see a small, starkly white cloud directly above my head, alone in an otherwise infinitely clear blue Arizona sky. As my breathing regulates itself, I track this cloud's changing form. In wonderment, I see it become the essence of all that he was to me. This is the answer I seek! Straining to send my own spirit heavenward to meet him, I'm caught between the constraints of Judeo-Christianity and the bare bones of sensation-based observance, a Buddhist meditation leaving me nothing but my own experience of impermanence, like the vapor that is this cloud above me.

I am seeking a sign, and this vaporous cloud looks amazingly like my husband to me. The search for signs is overwhelming in my grieving state. My need to make connections—and solidify them into my psyche—needs to fill the void, to repair the rupture. And just to be sure, I reach for my camera to capture the image that others might think was nothing more than my projected longing. I capture a comfort beyond anything they may ever understand or believe. This is private healing.

Time passes. Now the light is shifting with each passing cloud...the husband cloud long arched into the eastern sky. Shade-sculpted mountains seem to be moving toward me. Here the wind sounds like a highway at times, and at least twice a crystalline song bird reminds me that my husband, if I choose to believe it, is watching over me. This is what I came here to find. I feel soothed, bathed in the refreshment of this nature, whose air feels uncontaminated and pure.

April 28

Tonight I am again filled with possibility. The sky is filled with stars. I refuse to allow myself to indulge in romantic nostalgia. I now know my limits and how to avoid leading myself into self-pity. There is nothing attractive about it for me. There will be enough times ahead when despair and depression will descend upon me. Now, however, I am myself in the place of my choosing. I feel younger than my years. Spirit is ageless, I suppose. The kindness of strangers is immense. And the horizons for my life are as broad as my willingness to surrender my fears.

Dear Reader: In the midst of death, it is so important to keep faith with life and love. You are still alive, and you owe it to yourself and to the memory of your loved one to find reasons to keep your spirit healthy and strong.

No one can tell you when you will be ready to laugh again—when you will find joy and feel your step quicken. Only you will sense the beginnings of this gradual healing and making yourself whole. You may be tempted to deny this awakening, to push it away, feeling a terrible guilt that happiness—however fleeting—has returned so soon. I urge you to be kind to yourself. You are fragile and vulnerable, just as I was: like a virgin—a Virgin Widow.

There is a great temptation for our friends and relatives with mobilized protective instincts to impose or project their feelings upon us—we who are "victims of loss." Well meaning, they are inclined to treat us as wounded or in shock, with impaired or inadequate judgment, as if we do not know what's right for us, or as if they know better, or as if we shouldn't be left alone to think morbid, "self-sabotaging" thoughts.

My sense is that each of us needs different elements in order to become whole and thus to heal because we do have innate healing capabilities, and they vary with our personalities. For each of us, a healing environment can be defined in several ways, and we have survival instincts for those kinds of choices. I think perhaps it's more of a challenge to assert ourselves with our protectors than it is to be drawn into the darkness by our own tendencies.

And here are two questions, for here they arise: When *are* you ready to be with people? When *are* you ready to put your thoughts aside and pay attention to the minutiae of life? Though I decided to go back to work and get on with my routine very quickly, a part of me knew I was not fully ready one month later, when I felt myself drift away so easily and often in the midst of public gatherings. This may have been the reason I felt such a need to travel—to distance myself from the familiar and all its expectations of me—and surround myself with a newly minted canvas, one that held no guilt and offered endless opportunity.

Looking back on this decision to travel to a meaningful place in the month that followed my husband's radical departure, I am struck by how integral this journey was to my rebirthing process. My desire to visit places that we had shared, that were enticing for me while married, demanded to be revisited, to be informed of the change, and to be translated into my own experience of that alteration in life expectancy. There was something liberating about releasing the dream in the form it was held that allowed space for new dreams to emerge.

I felt lighter leaving Arizona, readier to return and face the inevitable reality of life without the security of a partner.

Chapter 4

Defining Transition Tools: Picking up the Pieces

Grief cultivates my soul
like a plough through soil.
I am furrowed and softened: a place
of fertility for seeds to grow,
and I am the farmer
offering fields for grazing and growth.
If there is utility in all this upheaval,
let it be useful to my world!

Grieving: It is a constant ocean of feelings. Thick and thin, dense and filmy. Grief comes and goes and in between is joy and excitement. Larvae of change swarming within. An internal tingling without the benefit of form. Just the promise of form. A quickening in the soul that carries with it an amorphous expectancy.

I walk around with this feeling as much as I walk with the heaviness of grief and the tears that spill down my cheeks without warning. Grieving is dynamic. It is like the forest floor: alive with every season and the cycle of growth and decay.

The days since my trip to Arizona have been admittedly brighter. The trip afforded a much-needed break—a chance to breathe and rebalance; to inhale and exhale under the wide open sky. Now I am back in a harness. Settling this estate. So careful. So fair. So excruciatingly conscious of details and calibrations. Walking this tightrope. This one foot in front of the other. Divisions. Lines of delineation. Documentation. Operating full force in a field that is not my strength and yet I must. Even with the help of a trusted advisor, it takes all of me, and my outcome is a growing, spreading, debilitating pain.

My body's strength has begun to unravel through all of this. Letting go of my daily commitment to a workout: building strength, keeping pain at arm's length. All the long hours bent over papers; holding in all the pent-up fear and restraint. Now I'm in constant discomfort. My left shoulder, my right scapula, my left lower back and upper thigh, the sciatic nerve pinched with the contractions of staying focused and accomplishing this push through the birth canal of "middlescence."

May 4

Trying to find what constitutes my new normal, I awaken to a cloudy day and mournful-sounding spring birds singing in a minimal and lonely key amid the grayness. When I arrived home, I didn't cry. I unpacked, watched TV—melting into the nothing world of that automatic action—and read a few pages before falling into an interrupted sleep.

Yesterday was a day of catching up and staying present. Today, my girlfriend has returned to help me sort and pack up more of Richard's things while I see clients and look forward to dinner with friends. I don't refuse any invitations. I try to stay open, though I still forget to relax. I get frightened of becoming ill from holding all the pain. A sunny day may make it easier. One can only hope.

May 5

Last night, I puttered till well after midnight with paperwork and computer correspondence until I was tired enough to retire. Reading a novel, I found myself riding the queasy waves of intimate emotional territory that is far too familiar for comfort.

To counteract my anxiety, I navigated toward my inner island of gratitude. I sent thanks for all that I have…

Dear God,

I am so grateful for my friendships, for my birthday reminders of all the ways I am blessed, and for my parents, so loving and alive.

I am grateful for my lovely home and for the comfort around me.

I am grateful for my helpers and for my potential.

I am grateful for my work.

I am grateful for the life I have, for living here and not in some crazy country where strangers come into your home and seize your life and loved ones for no reason except that they can.

Now it is time for my morning walk and then to shower and get ready for my day, to prepare for the clients who put themselves in my care. Later, I will write Arizona thank you notes and compose an acknowledgment to Richard's school community and to those who honored us with their outpourings of love and remembrance.

Later…

After 10:30 p.m., I've just returned from dinner with dear friends, a lovely time filled with good conversation. The earth is turning green, and I am feeling sheltered and cloistered. My garden smells like summer. It is a great comfort.

Serendipity feeds me. Staying in the here and now keeps me sane. Refraining from conjecture keeps me on an even keel. Staying busy keeps me in the zone of positivity and possibility.

Dear God,

I need to stay sane. Thank you for your blessings: beautiful birthday cards, good friends, and the love and protection that surround me. Caring people help me feel cherished and fortunate.

Life…we can never have it all at once. I was so loved by my husband, but sometimes that love separated me from the rest of the world. Now that I feel supported by my immediate world, I crave the exclusive brand of "husband love."

Dear God,

Let me be thankful for whatever is in my life. Let me love it as it is, with no conditions and preconceptions. Between you and me, God, this being without a mate is one of life's most difficult challenges. Allow me to rise graciously to the occasion...

Tears and more tears. How do I deal with this overflow of sentiment, this eye in the hurricane that is my life? How do I receive the love? How do I contain the emotions? How do I deserve all this? Who am I to deserve all this? Am I really so loved? What does it all mean? What is the meaning of my life? How many of us receive this avalanche of attentive support and caring in life? What is this about for me?

Dear God,

This is such a traumatic time...a time of great emergence, a time of great emergency, personally. Grant me the expansion to feel it all, to contain it and to learn from it. This is a time like no other. This is a time of tremendous grace, tremendous pain, and tremendous recognition. Please grant me the equanimity to use it wisely and to grow from within.

May 8

Early morning. I review a recent astrological reading, one of a series of annual readings that I have used to provide the widest possible perspective on the cycles of my life. I reflect upon my previous experiences under the influences of sober Saturn, that slow and heavy planetary force that requires us to deal with mundane details for such a long, unhappy time. How could that influence ever be truer than now? Each moment is oppressive, obsessed with details. An absence of glamour and an abiding presence of dull routine. And many more months of it await me. This is what we call a "dark gift"…

"In the end, through hard work and perseverance, we become increasingly adept in the area of our charted Saturn influences."

Endless paperwork was the bane of my husband's existence, and it has now fallen into my lap. Ironic. And temporary, I presume, but there is no end in sight from here. Now I get to understand the relentless pull that paperwork had on him, this illusion of control. I feel myself embodying his spirit as I remain committed to *this* task, *his* chair, and *his* space—all of these demand that I complete my duty until the wee hours of the morning. How familiar. How unnerving.

May 11

Dinner out with friends every night for the past three nights. I feel so fortunate that I have somewhere to go every evening and don't wind up alone. I'm so glad that I made this commitment to myself and didn't leave things to chance. My work is unlike so many careers; it is never about me. At the end of the day, I need that "me" time, when I can relate to others in a more social manner. With Richard gone, it is essential to share ordinary moments with people I love.

Nevertheless, I still come home to an empty house and let myself fall to the floor, crying my eyes out. Java cat circles cautiously, feathering me with his silky tail. He opens my heart and I cry harder. It is a Friday, and they are the most difficult days.

Fridays were always difficult anyway. My husband—the natural introvert—craved privacy after a week of being in performance mode, whereas I—the natural extrovert—craved stimulation after a week of being sequestered with my clients. Our energies and intentions would inevitably clash as our two distinct weather fronts collided. There would be disagreement and frustration. Now, there's another kind of torment: the absence of that predictable conflict. What I face now, again, is that tumultuous emptiness as the specter of another barren weekend approaches. Wonder and weirdness roll in.

May 12

Tonight, I am numb as I am facing a gigantic day tomorrow. Need to be out of here by 8:00 a.m. to get on with a full schedule of clients. It feels like my strategy is to knock myself out until I don't or can't care about anything else, being too tired, too occupied.

Another strategy is to schedule events and activities that will create new ideas, establish new networks, and develop new contacts. I need to plan my summer as well. Retreats are a learning experience, like emptying and refilling at the same time.

My work holds a particular gift for me in that I can plan on my own what might advance my expertise and benefit my clients as well. This is what I call a worthy combination of direction and distraction. Once I am established at these retreats, maybe I can meet some new people. Is this what it takes to bring myself back to equilibrium?

May 13

My future is unimaginable. There is a perplexity about this in my psyche as I am mostly used to imagining all kinds of futures. Instead, my consciousness is caught up in revisiting the past. My history seems to have a mind of its own. Personal videotapes of my life keep replaying themselves at random; snippets of adolescence, childhood, and everything else popping up despite minimal provocation.

From moment to moment, triggered by the slightest things, I am flooded with pictures. Part nostalgia, part regret—a bittersweet yearning for lost time, lost moments, and the fleeting, unappreciated fragments of life. Now, in their exquisite and frustrating irretrievability, lost forever to the unrelenting forward movement of my innocent intentionality, I am bereft. Like a shopping trip where nothing is "me" because "I" am nothing. Instead of panicking, I breathe deeply.

Just because I can't imagine my future doesn't mean it doesn't exist; it doesn't mean I don't exist. And it doesn't invalidate my present, either.

Dear Reader: Grief can be a slippery, uphill climb during which we reach for handholds that can anchor us in the midst of chaos. What may seem irrational to the outside observer—astrological readings; visits to mediums; writing letters to those we've lost; and frantic, often incoherent prayers—can comfort us when there is nothing else.

May 15

Comfort and security: Both of these needs swim around me like dolphins. It's completely up to me to provide these for myself. But hasn't it always been like this? What is the nature of the illusion that allows partnership to feel like any kind of insurance against pain?

I search for ways to comfort myself and seek methods to prevent / postpone / mediate / moderate / dissolve pain. Exploring my outer space: releasing the impulse to fuel my intellect for a flight to unexplored territory. Departing from known practices. Reading books I wouldn't necessarily have read in my other life. Listening to music that holds no reminders of the past. Home from work and I'm feeling restless.

My darling,

To have you gone and to be left with the least interesting parts of your life is intolerable. I miss the warmth of your touch, your animation, your velvety way, your compassion. How I miss you. Sometimes the feeling of loss threatens to suffocate me. I must remember to breathe. I get so angry. I feel so lost. My world is overrun with so many clichés.

There's no comfort for me in your things. Only in your image, at times, and in the wonderful memories that people so often mention in their condolence cards. "Let your wonderful memories be a comfort to you." But are they? Or do they taunt me with their irretrievability? Do they tempt me with their nearness to my heart? Do they sadden me because I will never live them with you again? Perhaps they will comfort me one day. Now they just feel cruel and elusive.

May 16

I am reorganizing from the outside in and the inside out. What I'm really doing is going through everything I own and deciding about each object… deciding what purpose it serves and then disposing of it. There is so much of me in my "everything" drawer and so much "stuff and nonsense," it makes me wonder at the clutter. What if I had died? How would anyone know what mattered? If any of this collection actually does. I take the time to sift through old wallets, pens, buttons, sewing kits from hotel rooms, faded receipts, little journals filled with odd notes, and more. It is a kind of cleansing that gives me purpose, a task; that keeps me from thinking beyond "keep" and "discard."

Today is different from last Sunday. Last week, I was high on connections and connecting. Today, I am feeling tired and empty and hollow. The day is lovely, fragrant, and mild. I could sit outside or walk among the flowers. But I'm exhausted. I should finish clearing another drawer. Just a few more minutes and then rest. That's a good idea. Rest and stop fretting.

Of course I don't. A friend calls, overflowing with news. What can I do? She's my friend, and I have to make her happiness my friend as well. And I do. But the discussion about Saturn to the nth degree I didn't need. In the midst of all this, it's too much. Two more years of misery ahead? There are so many better things to hold onto, to believe. And yet, the reality of Saturn is slow-moving sadness; a front that hangs on, not easily blown by the winds of change.

I remember a long-ago summer when the entire month of July was cool and rainy, and I was working with the hopeless and helpless. Every day was cloudy. Every day I wore a sweater.

Today the bitterness feels like soft dirt mixed with water: a kind of silty, sludgy mud that weighs too heavy on my heart. My eyes are pulled down at the corners like my mouth. My hair is freshly cut, but when I look in the mirror, I see such sadness that I feel pathetic. I feel like something discarded. Who does that make me now? Where does it leave me now? Who the hell *am I* now? How bitter this time is. And this isn't even the worst of it.

I take a deep breath. Forget the worst. The best of it is that I'm okay financially. I am in planning mode for my future. I am surrounded and supported with loving friends. I have my work already cut out for me. I don't have to guess what to do next. I only have to do it. And I have to take care of myself. Stay healthy. Make good choices.

If fishermen can't fish, they repair their nets. I will repair mine. I will nurture my friendships and stay open to the future. I will sow seeds and appreciate my blessings. I will have the best time I can with what I have. I will learn to be alone and appreciate myself. It has been two and a half months since his death: two and a half months of awakening to this next chapter of my life.

May 21

The children are here, going through boxes and mementos. I feel sick, on the verge of tears, heavy hearted. The revolving spectrum of loss: missing, yearning, longing...disorientation. Like a white-hot throbbing in my guts, the compact and secret agony of this emptiness rivets me to the past and to our unlived future. I struggle to stay present in the presence of his children, for whom this unspeakable pain is sharper now that they're here. My heart goes out to them.

Physically, no matter what I do, I don't look well to myself. I look contrived...like an old face in a new mirror. Who is this woman of the past looking back at me? I'm completely rearranged on the inside, and yet she appears as if nothing has changed. She isn't me now. But who is? How does "me" look today? How can my physical reflect my psychological? Impossible. Dismal.

Forecast: My mood is dark and cloudy with intermittent tearfulness. I suppose the "going through boxes" is like raising a kind of emotional dust in my space. Missing Richard, appreciating the life he lived before me, his character, and the making of it. How richly, in many ways, he lived his life. How passionately. How committed. How full of intention and follow-through. My man. A man who loved me so thoroughly and knew how to express it. Although I came after his true soul mate connection, which was his school.

Getting over this loss takes every ounce of consciousness I possess. It takes self-possession. This transition time. The disorientation... the dreading of winter, the excessive and self-protective planning, the yearning for what was, the self-deprecation regarding my lack of appreciation in the past, for what I *did* have. And after the mourning, there is opportunity for the new. How to seed myself with enough stimulation to even be inclined toward the "new." How will that ever happen? I must stay intentional. Try not to give into malaise and fatigue. Stay purposeful. Stay committed to my plans. One of these is the trip to Colorado. This is essential.

May 24

How fortunate is my work in that it addresses human suffering! And if character is destiny, how exercising it is for me to use this pain, like grist for the mill that grounds my daily practice of coaching and psychotherapy. Painful as it is, I carry an image of conversion. Grief cultivates my soul like a plough through soil. I am furrowed and softened: a place of fertility for seeds to grow, and I am the farmer offering fields for grazing and growth. If there is utility in all this upheaval, let it be useful to my world!

May 29

Running out of energy early. A haze of denied depression hangs over me and tinges my aura with grayness. I burst into tears while ironing and listening to oldies on the stereo. And yet I make the best of it...keeping myself numb. Anticipating the far end of this tragedy and projecting into unknown futures.

I'm edgy now. Every time the sun goes in, I feel soothed. Relief from the burning bright demand of the holiday weekend. Every time the sun comes out, I feel compelled to celebrate. And the mood of celebration is hard for me to generate. The central air conditioning is a godsend. As are the room-darkening shades in my bedroom.

As I get down to basics, my mood is pushed and pulled by the immediacy of the environment, the weather. The relief of cloudiness allows me to be blue or gray or neutral. The sunshine somehow demands my participation. It is so hard to ignore its insistent gaiety, especially this time of year. I am feeling progressively in sync and out of sync as the day moves through its partial cloudiness. In and out. In and out. Me too.

May 30

Life is very simple. Just rise and do. When darkness falls, I am unwilling to focus on tasks. I prefer to get into bed and read to fall asleep. In the light of day, I want to run away.

Later that night.

A first: out for dinner with friends, I'm surprised that I'm eager to return home and be alone. Feeling tired as well as a little headachy and missing the comfort of my cat. Oddly, I don't feel a sense of dread or even loneliness. Rather, I feel a sense of comfort and serenity about returning home. Allowing my cells to greedily expand to the limits of my aloneness, I am, on some level, hungry for my space. True, I also fear it, but true as well is that I'm only as alone as I desire to be. Voices are a phone call away. And, although I haven't yet tested it, there is an Internet site called Unexpected Angels for those who have lost their spouses, suddenly.

Beyond the exchanges with Jim Miller, I have not exploited the company of the Internet to any extent at all. And there is the West Coast if it gets too late here in New York to make phone calls. And I always have Java, curling willingly beside me.

But mostly there is a feeling of grace around me...around this time. Almost like a license to do whatever and be whoever makes sense to me. Call it a forgiveness of mood: a feeling of permission similar to being excused from obligation because of illness. The relief when one can simply spend the day in bed nursing a cold after needing a rest for months. I am relieved I don't have to do anything more than simply coast.

I just need to be wary of those thoughts that would torture me with prophecies promising an unfulfilled life as a widow. And of other superstitious kinds of non-productive speculation or planning. If I were to have anything, it would be—it should be—to have faith. In myself and in life. Needing to have the reminder in print, I have "FAITH" engraved on my favorite bracelet.

May 31

Of course, life is unfolding every minute. I sleep heavily, till almost 8:00 a.m., and I awake with the ongoing sciatic-type pain, reminded that I need an x-ray of my spine... How much I procrastinate. Ongoing maintenance. The car needs it too.

June 5

It's 11:30 p.m., and I'm up, still dressed, and I haven't yet gone upstairs to try to sleep. A charcoal gray malaise has been creeping into my fiber since yesterday afternoon, and I'm recovering from a day of trying to keep my head above water.

As I turned my key in the side door lock this evening, I had the bizarre thought that this was a Friday, and on most Fridays, we would fight in order to settle down for the weekend. We would usually make it through dinner and fight on the way home from the restaurant, but sometimes we would fight on the way *to* the restaurant. We would also find something—rather, *he* would find something—that would be the flint for an explosion on Friday night. Most times, we'd make up before sleeping, but often it would take a few hours. A few times, I slept in the other room, and once, I remember making plans to separate. I remember that I was going to live in a friend's beach house for the spring season.

So it occurred to me to make a list of all the things I do *not* miss about my husband. Maybe that would be a way of minimizing my self-pity and helping me keep perspective about the opportunity for another way of life that this tragedy of loss presents. So here goes:

- I do not miss fighting on Friday nights.

- I do not miss wasting hours fighting at all.

- I do not miss having him here but not having him at all.

- I do not miss his unreasonable demands.

The truth is, though, that I miss even his less attractive habits. I would give anything to have him back. And I don't want to cry.

June 11

Today was exceptional in many ways. I took the opportunity to experience Sarah's Fragrance Journey and create a perfume for myself. I named it "Expectancy 99" to pave the way for dreams that come true. Fragrance has always offered a special catalyst for me to revise my feelings. For me, the way that the olfactory nerve goes directly to the brain allows me to change my experience—my "felt sense"—in an instant. Connecting with Sarah, whom I've known since her childhood, contains the blessing of creativity and the promise of a shift in experience. With the fantasy of naming a fragrance comes the ability to *have* that experience. Expectancy: An accurate moniker for this time in my process of re-creation.

Now it's time to begin the night journey: to prepare for sleep and for a weekend well deserved. I face a big week, working as hard as I can to justify going away for two weeks in July and one in August. The life doesn't sound half bad.

New glimmers: For the first time, I allow myself to desire male companionship. Not to act on it. Just desire it. Truly. Honestly. And I allowed myself to think about moving to a condo. Just thinking about looking in the paper. Just thinking what it would be like. Just thinking of how a change in personal venue might benefit my healing.

I've begun examining books on leadership in business. Newness, in the form of thinking about consulting with businesses again. I appreciate my sparkling home. I appreciate my parents who are such parents...even now. I even think about getting a second cat.

Much later...

I am paralyzed with inertia. I have absolutely no inclinations. Can't even watch TV or read a book. I feel dysfunctional. Why can't I even read? It's almost as if I'm content to simply stare into space until it's late enough to go to sleep legitimately. And I'm not particularly crying or depressed in the classical way. Simply numb.

I did a stupid thing by buying a quart of ice cream and forcing myself to eat three servings that I didn't even want. I hate nights. Empty nights, especially.

Why can't I even get interested in speaking to someone online? Or watch TV? Killing time has always been illegal in my book, and now look at me. Why can't I do something productive?

Cool and cloudy, maybe a sprinkle of rain. Tomorrow, I should awaken early and plant my flowers. Less is more. I look forward to planting in the cool drizzle. Better walk off all of this ice cream, too. I need to look pretty for the memorial service. I will have my hair trimmed. When the time is right, I will rejoin the human race.

How is this alone time shaping me, reshaping me? How am I changing? Or not? How can I continue to have faith? How can I afford not to? What can I read? What do I need to learn? How do I need to expand, spiritually?

June 20

There is so much I'm thinking about. The tribute services I must attend. My work. And traveling. Travel is the most healing thing I can do. It puts miles between me and my old life. It crowds my mind with visions of the future, but, more importantly, it's laden with newness. With feelings and sounds and sights that demand all of my attention. It's consuming. It fills my crevices. It leaves little room for melancholy.

The Memorial: This morning, up early to prepare myself, to ground myself, and to feel connected to the warm spring day. The service will be outdoors to accommodate the large audience. I walk the neighborhood, mentally rehearsing. On the lawn of a retired librarian I barely know, there are a pair of white doves sitting still on the branch of an apple tree, not a common sight. In fact, I've never seen them before. Maybe it's the hour. Everyone still asleep; it's just dawn. So symbolic, and so fitting in so many ways.

The tribute service and all of its attendant parts facilitate a whoosh of movement on my path. I am proud of my ability to reach in deeply, to keep my heart open, to write and perform under conditions of extreme emotionality. The pressure to be "on" in front of so many watching, balanced against the need to sincerely grieve, creates a strange feeling that I am "acting" *and* "being." Two women in one body and yet terribly alone. It scares me a little. Yet even as it scares me, I'm aware of its potential to assist in forcing another layer of resolution to my simple acceptance of Richard's death. Not so simple. I feel a need to reach out to Jim Miller, my bereavement mentor, again.

Dear Jim, I write:

"This week was a milestone in that my husband's school district created a huge memorial/tribute service for him. My own feelings ranged from anxiety to relief as my role required me to speak on two separate occasions after some overwhelmingly emotional musical slide-shows recalling his professional life as a principal. I survived. Now I must allow myself to re-heal after the wound being all opened up this week. I have planned to travel to the Rockies for a writing retreat in July."

Hello, Andrea, he writes:

"Your time with the memorials for your husband sounds exhausting to me. Such experiences can be very important for people who want to express themselves, for communities that need healing. But they can also demand so much of the one who is in your position. Their timing may not coincide with your timing. A writing retreat in the Rockies sounds wonderful. Please stay in touch."

Dear Jim, I write:

"The retreat is being held at a convent near Colorado Springs. There will be 11 women from all over the country. The week is billed as a combination of writing, bodywork, nature walks, and nurturing cuisine. The theme is called *Graceful Passage: Staying Openhearted in Times of Change.* I am looking forward to it, anticipating the opportunity to gather myself in this soothing environment. I can think of no better way than with the distance of a retreat in combination with the support of like-minded strangers."

June 25

There is so much to catch up on I had to set aside special time here to set down, in writing, some of the unfolding.

First, I need to really acknowledge the presence and continuation of grace in my life. This life. This life alone but not lonely. This life full of change. This life full of possibility. I hardly know what to make of it. And, probably, I needn't try. It just is.

Deep awarenesses: I live in the present. I attempt to stay present. I try not to think of the future. The future is too abstract...too unthinkable. If I think of the future, then I think of the future I won't ever have. All that future we planned together…working together, researching, writing, and publishing.

I will have some other future. But in that future I will be different, and I don't yet know what that looks like but I know I am in charge of creating that.

With gratitude, I am feeling self-sufficient. I am feeling enough. I am feeling as though I have what I need, right now, to survive…even to live well. I come home at night and turn on the computer. I communicate with the outside world exponentially, pushing at the limits of my life in order to reshape my direction. To live in the "no longer" is anathema to me.

My world has expanded. People know my situation and reach out to me. They reach into my mail, they drop me cards, they call on the telephone, and, out of the blue, they invite me places. And I say yes. I go. I visit. I attend parties. I write back. I make plans. My life has vitality.

The days since the tribute service have been admittedly lighter. The ceremony was a passage of sorts. The accumulating anxiety was like midsummer heavy thunderclouds gathering humidity and haze. Piling up, the self-control built to towering heights inside my psyche and exploded inside my cells, which—to this day—hold onto the incredible tension produced by the process. Memorializing a life and sharing in front of hundreds. So exposed. So public. So necessary.

I am holding onto my commitment to enjoy, to relish, to appreciate, to rediscover things that make me smile, and to give myself permission to celebrate them. I'm looking forward to giving myself some time away: To attend the workshop in Colorado; to visit close friends in California; to go to the retreat in Arizona. How can I do this? Do I have a false sense of financial security? Is it that I am feeling entitled to invest in myself, to invest it in ways that allow me to explore my horizons? To see what I can do with my work and my network?

My home is beautiful: a safe haven; a sanctuary. But is it essential to the life I see for myself in the future? How do I see that life? How do I see me?

Mostly, I need to create a schedule to get my strength back. Start with daily yoga practice and with stretching. I need to be more disciplined, as I've always promised myself, as I've always done in the past. Tomorrow, I have ten hours of patients. How do I fit "me" into that?

Dear Reader: By now, you will have realized that much of this guide illustrates *the way that I dealt with grief,* how it is *my* character to take on this adversity as an opportunity to evolve.

Throughout my journal entries, there is considerable "self-talk"—part pep talk and part permission, reporting back to my "internal Board of Directors"— which is my way of clarifying and convincing myself that the steps I am taking are right for me.

It is not my intention to have you do as I have done— or as any others would have you do—but rather to know you have the right to follow your own path.

Because of my profession, and because I have learned from my clients, I expect life to be difficult. I don't mean this as negative, only realistic. The choice we have is to exercise our ability to make use of the task before us as nourishment for that strength. This is a decision *that I make* that helps *me* see opportunity for healing, even in the darkness. I choose this belief as I would choose to go down a tree-lined street rather than a dirt road or a freeway. The important thing to remember is that *we all choose differently* based upon our uniqueness.

I'm comfortable as a mostly extroverted person. Under stress, lost, or confused, I prefer the company of others. You may need more alone time to heal. What matters is knowing what is right for you and making your preferences clear by being true to yourself.

If you have some resources—as I did—and you have the opportunity to be good to yourself, my advice is to act on it and leave the second-guessing to someone else. After all, this is one of the direst times in life, the proverbial rainy day everyone talks about. What you invest now, in yourself, will come back to you multi-fold. The self-affirming decisions will ultimately lead to a stronger you. This is how we shape and rebuild ourselves during our time of healing. This is not the time to be stingy.

As you are coming to realize, the stages of grief are not neatly defined. We do not transition smoothly from one to the next, leaving each separate, tidy phase neatly closed behind.

In the weeks before my husband's tribute services, I was overwhelmed by conflicting emotions that threatened to undo the good, healing work I'd begun. Though yours may not be as public, the very act of stepping into the world each day, going to your place of work, accepting the condolences of friends and coworkers, and dealing with the social niceties that never go away will be a test of your inner strength. This will exhaust your defenses when you least expect it. But you will make it. One step at a time. Day by day. And you will come to realize— as I did—that being forced to "perform" expected functions will help you to "actually" reintegrate yourself into your world.

TURNING POINT

Early July: I'm in Colorado, and there's such a feeling of relief even as I step off the plane. Somehow, the change in atmosphere is translated into a kind of freedom in my body. The air feels lighter, almost easier to breathe, although the elevation should make it feel just the opposite. The slant of the sun, the rise of the mountains, and the subtle fragrances of pine lift me with them. What a comfort to anticipate time with a childhood friend, all strengthening my original Self—my Self before marriage—in a place that has nothing to do with any part of the past decades.

There's this way I experiment with excising the death and loss... if I connect the before with the after... to dull the sharpness of the pain. (If I construct a mantra to remember, it is that I *did* have a life before this marriage, this relationship, and I *will* have a life after. It *is* possible.)

I am cherishing many moments in this time of safety and sanctuary. The reassurance of being with someone who knew me then and knows me now. Seeing my "self" reflected back to me in the eyes and heart of a decades-long friendship where there can be no hiding with this sister/friend who will always see the girl in me. Our laughter and relentless honesty keep me young and refreshed, remove my cynicism, and widen my vision like the long hikes up the foothills of the Rockies. I feel bathed and soothed with youthfulness, prepared to move from this cherished familiarity to the challenging unfamiliar.

With the feeling of being ferried from my personal angel to angels unknown, we drive together to Colorado Springs, where I am deposited at the gate of a retreat house to take part in a program with the theme of "Graceful Passages." How could I resist a title like that? The feeling of being among strangers without a story that draws attention gives me permission to simply be…the beauty of being in a spiritual place…the silence and the validation.

The writing retreat sandwiched between visits with close friends makes this trip one of the most satisfying in a long time. There's a balance of social exchange and solitary rumination; lots of time for silence, reflection, and (consequently) healing. There are handfuls of chocolate Dove pieces to grab from a huge bowl as we exit the main session and go to our rooms. Before registering, I made sure I would have a private room, and the pleasure of this separation is blissful for me. Being alone in the presence of others feels perfect; safe and secure yet stimulating of fresh perspectives.

As I sit in the sacred writing circle, I feel the shifts inside my psyche. Being there as me and not particularly as a widow allows my internal light to shine more strongly, and I feel my life-force gathering its momentum. I feel renewal in the making.

July 30

Back in my regular life, I cherish the time spent out West, and it's clear that my mission is to organize myself to create time to be away from here—where I live and work—developing, learning, and meeting people. Living well without a male partner in my life or on the horizon, as well as the summer heat, has kept me close to the comfort of home and the shade of my garden. I am getting used to and appreciating moving in my own rhythm.

The sensuality of my flowers, their color and fragrance; my aesthetic environment; the touch of my nails on the computer keys; the comfort of my young cat, Java, circling silky fur around my naked ankles—all this soothes me and keeps me savoring the moments, grateful to be privileged to be alive.

I live for being exposed to new friends and new futures.

All that is Hope twinkles with a soft seduction, unformed and unknown.

Even the possibility of male companionship glitters like the water's surface somewhere in the distance, the sparkle more attractive than actuality at this point.

July 31

I've created a storehouse of energy fueled by my desire to offer my own retreat for women in transition this coming January 2000 in Arizona: Think, plan, do. It occurred to me as I left the Colorado writing retreat, and I tested out the idea on a few of my clients. Each one I asked expressed an interest. Now I have to secure a venue and keep the ball in play. Just the planning itself and all that stems from it instigates movement within me. Creation feels equivalent to living with purpose. This internal process is a great comfort. It keeps me feeling in charge instead of at the mercy of life's unfolding.

The past two days I have been overeating, but up until now I have been pretty good about food and moderately good about walking (although these days have been too hot for much of that). I am not yet in the routine of working out with weights or doing yoga. Maybe it's time for some Pilates to get myself back, literally, in the groove. Living "forward" has become a compulsion for me.

I look at the clock. I must get dressed. I've been invited to a party, and I've made the commitment to go. I imagine I'll be home early, too tired for much aside from crawling into bed.

Hours later, I come into the house, seal myself into its boundaries with the burglar alarm, turn the air conditioning on low, listen for the familiar starting spurt of the sprinkler system, and get into bed with another in a long line of books about change and transition. Studying gives me a sense of orientation, some semblance of "control." This tendency is an old one that harkens back to my days as a student.

I'm more comfortable with "student of change" than with "widow." Now if Java the cat would only learn to sleep peacefully with me instead of having so much night activity, I could feel contained and complete on this simple summer night.

August 10

I don't look back if I can help it, and when I cannot help it I hold my breath, as if that will stem the tidal wave of thickening emotion that threatens to overwhelm me at a moment's notice. Only then do I remember to breathe deeply, slowly, as in birthing— to make room for the chapter of memories that signified my marriage and all the days and weeks and months of my time with him. I make room for the beauty and the sorrow and the regrets and the bittersweet recollections of life's fruits and frustrations. A decade and a half with a man who taught me more about committed love than anyone I've known. I weep as I write this.

August 30

The issue of male companionship seems less important than I imagined it would. I feel there are more to choose among than ever before. As if I can have one if I really want one. But right now, it's not what I want. I want to heal myself, body, mind, and soul, first. Female friendships are the most nurturing right now.

Being alone is not so bad. Not only that, I kind of like it. It's relaxing. And I find myself steadier of mood, sturdier of emotion than I've been in a long time. Solitude, once terrifying, feels safe, even cozy. I am at peace with myself although I don't have things squared away yet. Even though I'm running back and forth between two offices—mine for my work, his for the estate settlement—I feel positive about the outcome. It's a big house, and I'm gradually spreading out, taking a larger form within my domain. The den will be where I hang out in winter. I may even put a little writing desk in the living room so I can use the fireplace while I write. For the first time, I am beginning to feel grounded, to feel safe in the actions of reconfiguring my world.

Dear Reader: The notion of turning points is certainly a gift of retrospect, but we can also feel them announcing themselves when we pay attention: Some of them may be subtle; others brash. I found that I could detect their oncoming presence by my inclinations and attractions—the ability that some things had to pique my interest, or to feel "just right." As if parenting my own inner teenager, I am on the lookout for opportunities that seem to have the potential for exposing me to experiences that speak to my strengths yet stretch me, too.

Chapter 5

Building a New Foundation: Choosing to Move Forward

I think we could all use a
"Bride's Guide to Widowhood:
What All of Us Should Know Before
We Depend on a Husband."

September 9

Today is the infamous six-month mark. Six months in the new life. He is in another place in my heart. In certain ways, I have created movement in my own life to keep out of the abject misery of it all, although in other ways, surprisingly I feel closer to him in death than I even did in life. I've introjected his compulsivity and need for attention to the details of life. Now, I am the bottom line.

September 20

I am self-consciously walking through the change and transition process. At the urging of my accountant, I have joined a women-in-business group whose theme is *Re-envisioning Your Business*. When given the opportunity to share, I realize that I have no energy for visions right now. If anything, I feel like the embodiment of *anti-vision*. My aching heart craves the darkness of solitude; my rational self pulls me into the light of social interaction. Though many choices and possibilities spin around me, I don't have the energy to connect with any of them fully.

October 1

My mind wanders. A major theme in my daydreams is running away from home. I do my required work, being with clients and patients, and then I attempt escape in as many real ways as I can.

Everything they say about this stage of the healing process is true. The first six months are filled with lots of adrenaline, lots of people around you. The wound is fresh, and you're in survival mode. I recall living in a state of grace and gratitude for all I did and do that contributes to my identity and security. Echoes of this still surround me, along with much darker feelings, like anger with myself for not knowing more about will preparation and tax implications. Anger and blame come back to ignorance, and I don't do well with not having been smart. I struggle with this. (Wryly, I think I should write *The Bride's Guide to Widowhood: What All of Us Should Know* Before *We Depend on a Husband.*)

Ironically, my practice is going through an ending cycle of its own, and I am grieving the need to say good-bye to clients who are finished with their present work but love coming to visit. I must gently end these relationships in all the appropriate ways, knowing there will be SPACE and VOID, both highly threatening. My impulse is to FILL

THE VOID. I get driven to make plans to regain a foothold with networking, knowing that I'm too unfocused and a kind of tired for which I don't have words. I can still think up brilliant ideas, but I have little energy for follow-through because I lack the time to truly organize and mobilize. Of course, I'd have time if I stopped running away in all the ways I do from the scary SPACE. But anxiety is very seductive.

I know that I should just sit in the emptiness and recognize that winter is arriving, and with it, hibernation. Hibernation is appealing, although not my usual thing. I prefer to sign up for lessons that take me in new directions (away from the VOID). For me, self-development is always good, when it's mixed with travel. This is my favorite brew.

October 20

Many choices and possibilities spin around me. I don't have enough energy to connect with any of them fully. My practice is still at low ebb, and yet I have decided to go back to Arizona between Christmas and New Year's.

How dare I think of going away for three weeks? And yet, how could I not? If I have faith in anything, it better be this process about which I give counsel every day of my life, to others.

Best-case scenario, my trip to Arizona functions as a vision quest of sorts. Maybe I'll come back with plans to work at something totally new. Maybe I'll be exposed to unimaginable inspiration and integrate new elements into my existing life. Infinite possibility awaits, mostly in the morning, when I'm fresh.

November 3

Feeling a little numb—can't really connect with purpose. Last night, I was too tired to get clear on my vision. Feeling very passive. Now it is bordering on a feeling, a dread of inadequacy, and yet I know my vision and intuition will return. Have faith.

November 5

Time for a new journal. Maybe time for a new way of journaling. Sometimes, simply changing my personal writing book, style, font, or colors rejuvenates me. Artificial, like a geographic cure. It interrupts habit patterns nonetheless, and changing habits is important now.

The Millennium is coming: I seek and find evidence of larger change all around, and that identification helps me feel less alone because it is a change for all of us, a millennial change.

Coming to accept the upheaval and changes in my own life. Learning to sort them. Breathing through them. Seeing the despair and disillusionment as part of the debris floating around me after the destruction. De-structuring my life, and life at large.

November 19

I have a date! A mini date, really: dinner and then a jazz group at a local bookstore. I'm a little nervous and yet looking forward to it. He's divorced. It feels as if this could be time spent with a very dear friend with undertones/overtones.

November 20

Things heat up quickly. Do I take the first man who comes along after my husband's death or do I listen to my circle of advisors and wait, experiment, write ads, explore far and wide? We had a lovely dinner.

We sat close. He touched my hand. He kissed me, and I knew this could lead to more. I got scared. It felt too rushed. I put an end to it. I feel confused.

December 20

Arizona: It's such a relief to be here, again. Could I become like those others who came here to visit... and stayed? It's just that I'm not ready to join my newly configured life back east...yet. I want to stay here. I feel like I'm five years old and I don't want to go home. I hear my inner child: "NO. I'm NOT going. Leave me alone. Leave without me!"

And so the New Millennium begins. Change is all around me, like it or not!

Chapter 6

Honoring the Process:
A Celebration of Discovery

Gratitude is exquisite awareness
imbued with grace.

To live with vitality, we need grounding. Acute awareness
affords a kind of stability that stays on like a light in a closet
during disorienting times. A natural response occurs when
we try to get our bearings after the shocking discovery that our
spouse has died. It is almost reflexive, a sort of anti-decimation

strategy after what feels like our life has been destroyed. This practice is akin to accounting: counting one's blessings, taking stock, making an inventory of what remains.

The Montauk Point Retreat - Teaching what I've learned has always helped me solidify my own learning and embody my experience. The process of giving back is a way of metabolizing life on a spiritual level: ingesting the wisdom and experience of living through a change, observing what works to facilitate that process, and codifying it and giving it back to people who are on their own journeys of discovery. In January, in those first days of the New Millennium, I host a gathering of people who are facing the challenge of change, of one sort or another. True alchemy, turning experience into wisdom and paying it forward.

February 5, 2000

Reflections looking back:

- ✎ I am grateful that my husband died quickly, with mere seconds of conscious suffering.

- ✎ I am grateful that he didn't suffer, that his death wasn't violent, that he had his affairs in order.

- ✎ I am grateful that he died in the presence of someone who truly cared for him and about him, someone with whom he had a good respectful relationship.

- ✎ I am grateful that I could be reached easily to be notified and that I could reach the children within minutes and have them arrive as soon as possible.

❧ I am grateful for the small insurance policy my husband had recently arranged and that my step-daughter remembered.

❧ I am grateful for my family around me.

❧ I am grateful for friends who formed a ring of protection and healing energy around me.

❧ I am grateful that I could and did work and that there was and is a meaningful place for me to show up and make a difference.

❧ With the relentless awareness of life's fragility, I am grateful to be alive and healthy and capable of creating life from here.

❧ I am grateful to be in possession of my gifts and talents and to know who I am in this world.

❧ I am grateful that my identity doesn't end with this death.

❧ I am grateful for the fertility to birth myself anew.

March 9 ... Again

Today I visited Richard's grave. Spring has arrived. Such sharp contrast to last year's storm, when thick snowflakes covered this entire cemetery with a blanket of insulation so sorely needed then. This year, the ground is warm, and I can set up a chair by his side and have a decent conversation with him.

March 10

I am evaluating events and resources on both conscious and unconscious levels for their sacred worthiness in making a difference in the realm of my personal security. People, places, and ideologies are twirled into the mix. Kaleidoscopically, the elements of life present and arrange themselves as each moment is poised and then falls upon the other, unfurling new layers of awesome recognition as new "reality" emerges from the husks of the old.

March 11

A new gray depression setting in like a storm front on the horizon. The constant demand of negotiating my moodiness is draining and leaves me exhausted. It must be the dark pull of this sad anniversary working through me. And just last week I thought I was doing fine. I tell myself to feel it, and not to get scared. Just go with it.

March 15

I am attempting to write in bed while a real maelstrom begins to wind itself into the neighborhood, promising downpours in the early hours of this upcoming morning. Sipping sherry and using my laptop for the first time since my "rest cure" in Arizona, I sense a newness brewing: a novelty in being alone, of sorts. A feeling of isolation and a distinct pleasure in feeling something different than in previous times: a little safer, a little cleaner, and a little scary in its maturity. As if I've always known that one day, this kind of life would be expected of me—required, in fact, as a matter of aging. And yet paradoxically this whole experience of grieving has me feeling so young.

I'm too awake to sleep, too lazy to clean and organize. It's too late to chat, too brimming with every slight new green movement within me to ignore myself. Is it possible that I am for the first time tasting singularity and allowing myself to relish it? What is the fear all about? The fear of liking it so much that I will never again be willing to give it up, to be able to join with another? The fear of *this* being *it,* so to speak? That *this* is all there is? That *this* is my life?

And what is this? It's a deep sense of peace, of serenity. A doing whatever I please. It's having a work life and a personal life of my own choosing. It's having my own interests—the easy ability to go places and to do things without compromise. And in the midst of this exotic sense of freedom, it's a kind of strange accountability: to dear friends and companions, to be sure, but mostly to myself. Is it too frightening to be accountable to no one but myself? Indeed, it is an unusual feeling, and this is an unusual time.

March 20

A big envelope from the IRS, pages full of complicated legalese. I finally manage to decipher the news that certain complicated aspects of negotiating the NYS retirement plan have been successful. My emotional response should be elation. Instead, I cry copiously.

This is the odd thing about times of change and transition. We can diligently work day after day to take care of survival and security needs, and yet once accomplished, we are left with the feeling that can only be described as tear-worthy: that mixture of sorrow and pain and fatigue and self-indulgent self pity and the soft reality that something once alive is finally and irrevocably gone. The unit, the relationship, the quality of couple-hood, along with its illusion of permanence, of insurance...no longer there. An entity, a conceptual container for life forever altered. Disappointment and disillusion overwhelm. The opportunity for something else to happen is my only buoy.

There is nowhere to go but different.

The question is, do we wait for circumstance to alter this space at the end of a radical disconnect? Or do we accept responsibility and begin to assemble options for the future? The emotions that accompany these thoughts feel like a gray, slow, churning, lonely oceanic expanse where the horizon and the sea are impossibly blurred beyond our reach. So, if the problem is that we want to see it and we can't, what's a human to do? I search myself for all the creativity I can muster for comfort.

March 21

Today is the official beginning of yet another season. Another spring unfolds before me, and I am alone except for my quiet mind and melting heart.

No interest in writing. Yesterday was too emotional. A hot, burning pain in my leg kept me up half the night. Today I am too busy to feel. I know I am just getting through the days, existing on minimal effort. No real joy. Should I be medicated for depression, or should I change the way I am thinking about my life?

March 24- Warwick, NY

Stretching before me, a panoramic view of early spring fields alive with nesting birds, grazing quarter horses, and freshly budding fruit trees. In the remaining daylight, clumps of daffodil and iris have already sprung up. Every species is nesting. The sound of a deep wind chime of kitchen utensils in the breeze. The raucous sound of boys playing fastball in the neighboring yard breaks my reverie.

March 29

The neutral zone. In search of another life. Needing, desiring love and passion. Wishing to have romantic love in my life again. I so want that feeling again. I have toyed with the idea of being rescued from this time and place. Fantasy: A bold knight; a renaissance man; a rebel who acts on impulse; someone to take me away from all this regular life now so highly irregular.

March 30

Let there be an end
to the whining
to the wishing
that life be
otherwise
Let there be an
appreciation
a dedication
to the life that
is—as is
There are worse fates than
being without a love that tears
at the heart
that turns breath into sobbing
silent in the dark
The stillness of a single life
pulses and grows
a pinpoint of glow
as
a new day breaks

April 13

I am consumed with feeling "normal" again, and I strain to think about what that means. How can I re-create what I used to take for granted? Why is being "uncoupled" through widowhood such an alien state and so aversive? Going to movies with friends, throwing out clutter, reorganizing closets and cupboards, planting herbs and spring flowers, initiating life in botanical form, I plan imaginary trips in my mind. Trying to keep myself afloat. Maybe a cruise?

April 15

I realize that if I am to move forward, I must let go of the "wife" archetype and embrace something new. With none in sight, I have the recurring idea that I need to be rescued and removed—abducted, in other words—and taken someplace I cannot reach on my own. Maybe someone else has a better idea.

April 18

Another very down day, except for the few hours where I'm engaged with my clients, and I lose myself in the meaningful intimacy of the therapeutic relationship: theirs and mine. Other than at work, I have a hard time pretending I'm OK. Mostly I'm so withdrawn that I can hardly even force a smile; to do so actually hurts my face.

My mood finally breaks tonight as my massage therapist works her magic. She is such a special person, such a funny lady, and the healing aspects of touch are so profound that I forget myself and wind up giggling with her. Between her skill and her comedy while she works, I feel... better! Thank Goddess!

April 20

Trying to respond to a sense of possibility instead of being pulled into the darkness of despair I go to see Dr. Robert in hopes of something— a magic bullet? A great mixture of feelings as I, a mental health practitioner, confide in a trusted psycho-pharmacologist. I feel alternately angry, disappointed, judging this to be a waste of time. He doesn't think I should rush into anything. But maybe his opinion is a blessing in disguise. Maybe his belief in the transiency of this state can serve as a life raft as I move forward in the molasses of this malaise. Maybe...

April 21

At a team meeting in my office with a group of colleagues. At first, I go through the motions, but soon enough I am caught up in the excitement of a professional endeavor with people I enjoy. It feels "normalizing" to be a part of something, to be useful. I feel a sliver of hope entering this dark abyss that has become my cave.

April 25

The rain and wind are seriously picking up. I read my journal from 1984: a summer of delusion and discontent manufactured out of my need to avoid the reality of my disappointing life back then. Two years before I would meet my husband, I struggled with such pain. I read now so that I may learn, so that I avoid this deadly ground again. How difficult and traumatic it was. How being without a partner seemed so intolerable. How illusion saved me and how, when my illusions were dissolved, I was bereft, wanting to end my life. Recognition brings hope. This time is different. Today, I am stronger.

April 29

I've chosen to spend my birthday on a flight to Denver, hoping to lose myself in the diversion of a professional development conference about, of all things, couples therapy. It is valiant for me to come here, courageous always to travel alone and to allow the adventure a sense of primacy and purpose in my life. I am here to improve clinical skills that are already pretty advanced and yet could always use some sharpening...a rather dull and blunt pencil these days.

I need to compensate for my lack of vitality. Perhaps feeding my head will help. I suppose it's wise to play to your strengths when you are feeling low on charisma. I suppose I could see this time as an opportunity to grow myself to become more developed and differentiated.

Right now, I don't have the intelligence, patience, fortitude, strength, or psychic energy to follow a thought or argument all the way through. Better to stay in the background and absorb rather than be in my usual center stage position. Nobody here knows me anyway, and so there are no expectations. Lots to be said for "remaining a stranger" when you're feeling strange.

During my morning (mourning) walk at 6:00 a.m., the early light and breezes are full of promise. A thought occurs to me:

I have this feeling that each man in my life has illuminated different sides of my being, my essence. I do not have a lover, so a whole side of me is left in shadow. And so it is now, a whole side of me like the dark side of the moon.

May 8

One of those breaks in my work day when I lose myself in the few minutes I have alone: those impossible few minutes when I feel so lost and irretrievable. Drowning, suffocating, and suspended. All at once! This horrible feeling of limbo accompanies a few moments of relative purposelessness. Not to be working is deadly for me. I want to lie down somewhere like a cat in a sunbeam—to be relieved of being human.

I reach into my pocket and find scribbled on a slip of yellow paper, torn off a larger pad, the beginnings of a personal ad: [I want...] "someone capable of spanning the emotional spectrum from old-fashioned romantic to modern, futuristic, and evolved..." As I connect to what I want instead of mooning over what I've lost, somehow something tiny releases in me—like a cough, and a deep breath.

May 18

Last night, I had a dinner out with my late husband's friends from work. Loving as they are, this is terribly disorienting for me. Where is my husband? Why isn't he here with us? I come home numb. All I want to do is get into bed and sleep until I'm transported to another lifetime.

Solitude is a salve. I want to talk to myself from a spiritual place of allowing the purposeful isolation of this time to be gentle and growth promoting. I've seen the relentless and judgmental side of me cajoling me to action and recovery while all I want is to be soothed. I'm trying to keep myself focused on gratitude—for my clients, for my friends, for my work and my cats, for this blessed time of empty nest—with potential. I talk to myself out loud as if I were advising my clients: "Just stay curious and willing to explore. Life's not over yet, even though it feels that way."

May 25

Awakened by thunderstorms, I get up to close the windows. Now, the challenge is to fall back to sleep. The middle of the night is such a narrow time in the psyche, such a fertile time for doubts and demons.

At 7:00 a.m., I'm awakened by the chime of my clock and the shining of sun—so rare these days. I'm aware of the absence of doom and the presence of a rather calm, stable feeling. I call for my kitten. She's comfortable, doesn't want to be disturbed, all stretched out on the headboard of the bed in front of the window. I invite her to me by patting the blanket. She complies, circling and finally backing into my chest. We spoon, her tiny, warm body a huge comfort, her silky hair fragrant under my chin. I speak softly of my love to her, for her. She turns and circles again, washing my cheeks with her raspy tongue. The peace of small wild things...

May 26

A friend's party, a crystalline night. I feel alive and vibrant: a glass of white wine, a great night, full enjoyment—so new, so renewed. I look pretty, feel pretty, stay pretty. Coming back to life?

May 27

I drive into Manhattan with anticipation. Early, no traffic. I'm excited about a professional meeting. I give myself to the leisure of an uncommonly relaxed morning on the West side, in Chelsea. I do breakfast alone at a sidewalk cafe. Meeting new people whose work I admire. I'm looking to synergize and create community with like-minded others, to be sourced by novelty and to contribute to an endeavor larger than myself...

Dear Reader: Sharing life with a significant other can create in us a kind of immunity against feelings of insignificance. When death robs us of our partner, it becomes startlingly obvious that we've built our security on a reflected sense of self. Helpless to stop it, we can do nothing but watch as our constructed illusions of safety, security, and sanctuary collapse.

From this perspective, it is easy to see how and why we experience feelings of "falling to pieces," "falling apart," or, in the worst-case scenario, "falling into the abyss."

Knowledge is power. Understanding the inclination to use our intimate relationships to keep emptiness and fear at bay can make us stronger. In the midst of recovery and reconstruction, this awareness provides a scaffolding upon which we can cling while feeling disconnected from life as we knew it. It offers a bridge from the ominous emptiness of the now to the faint glimmerings of hope in the future.

Our tribal nature demands that we create family where the primary nurturing structure once provided for our sense of who we are. When that is gone, it is our responsibility to fill the gap. We might get tripped up by or feel entitled to self-pity, but this leads nowhere fast. Our significance is a social matter—whether that is a small "s," as in our friendships, or a big "S," as in heroic pursuits. The bottom line is that we have to find a raison d'être.

Here, at this turn of the century, my own small change becomes dwarfed and yet validated by a historic moment. There is something deeply touching when a world event mirrors a moment in our own inner turmoil. It is this resonance that makes us feel that we are not alone.

Although we know that all pain eventually transforms and that Time heals, in the moment, the experience itself feels timeless. And sometimes we hold onto the grieving because it is our only connection to the one we have lost. To let go of the pain threatens us with letting go of the person.

Chapter 7

Creating Community: Finding A Place in the World

Defensively, I pack life very densely, incubating something. Life rotates slowly around me; the collection of people and experiences fills my time and my heart daily until I can again carry my own sense of self with more continuity.

June 5

I let myself get talked into going to the Tony Awards, a gift of tickets from one of my clients. I borrow the enthusiasm of two good friends, and although my companion is nice, he reminds me of a fast boy from my high school days: too quick with his words, his hands, his money; it's a lot of too much. Not a chance he can really communicate with or understand me. Inside, I'm tight and unreachable. In the end, despite it all, I'm glad I went.

June 12

Like a change in the weather pattern, all of a sudden life opens up. Newness everywhere. Where I was immobilized with depression and anxiety, now I am untethered, driving into Manhattan a few days this week, following the energy of the place, meeting old friends, and making new contacts. A flurry of dates to which I'm more or less numb and reserved on the inside, but I'm charming enough in demeanor.

I get away with it. I can pass for "interested and interesting." My job is to do "diligence" to push my limits, to explore, to challenge myself, to grow, to say "yes" to life, to try new things, to let go of the old ways, to embrace new patterns, to not be alone, to go out on blind and not-so-blind dates, to meet, to greet, to stay curious and attractive, and to celebrate love and friendship wherever I can (And remember to breathe!). To make the best of everything, to make small movements when I can, and to make progress and appreciate each little step. Like today, taking care of the details of life, tending to the droll necessities of keeping up the property, complying with regulations, dealing with the financial intricacies of the estate settlement, learning math, doing percentages, and dividing things equitably between my step-children and myself.

Father's Day, our anniversary

One of those perfect days. Planting flowers and getting caked with mud and sweat, I take a cold shower and then hold a festive brunch to celebrate that all of us are alive and well: Mom, Dad, my brother, my sister. I love my home today. I've made it mine again: beautiful, safe, and commodious. So exhausting is this preparation, and so rewarding. Planting every little seedling in hopes of a new flowering. Now, after the day is done, it rains gently, steadily. No thunder and lightning, no "sturm and drang"; rather, a cleansing, refreshing evening rain. I fall into a blissful sleep, petal after petal, ever opening within, a lotus emerging from sodden ground.

I dream of my husband. I call him at work. I don't reach him on the phone, but within moments, he comes into our bed and sleeps with me. Somewhere inside, I know he'll come if I call him. I am reassured.

July 1

I have been wanting to start a new journal volume, because, the truth is, I have felt an actual shift in my mood and in my perspective. I've been lighter, less morose, less consumed with what I don't have and more focused on what I do have. My security is within myself. At least, at last, I have me again, more solid and dependable than at any time in the last year and a quarter!

Dear Reader: Even in the midst of my darkest sorrow, grieving the loss of all that had been, the deepest part of me knew that I was not ready to give up, that I was not done with living, that I had more to give and would one day love again. This may not be where you find yourself now. But it will come. Life can't help but evolve. It is the nature of all things to change.

Chapter 8

Looking Back: Growing Stronger

*Who can explain the ways in which life
works with death and death with life?*

March 9, 2005

March 9, 1999 was a Tuesday morning wet with
yesterday's snow, the unrelenting kind that falls

freely and sticks only on the edges of leaves and grasses, outlining the natural world as a reminder of nature's power to discern what's important. This was the snow that fell on the funeral five years ago, on the day that we all had to admit that he was really gone. I revisit his final resting place now—a place I can locate like a homing pigeon in the midst of all those other resting places, distinct from all those other slumbering neighbors none of us knew. I took comfort then in the shape of the trees and the close protectiveness of shrubs and a stone wall that anchors the energy so there's no drifting in the endless sea of graves.

Now it's five years later, a gray and damp Tuesday morning. It is the first time that March 9th falls on a Tuesday again and I remember the last goodbye and the morning conversation back and forth upstairs to downstairs and downstairs to upstairs as we readied for our day. Words transported between us on different floors, preparing for our different lives, knowing we'd reunite at night, as usual. But by mid-morning, the bell had tolled. The ominous ringing of a phone at an unusual hour, in an unusual way, and nothing is usual again. Not for a very long time and maybe not even now, in certain ways. And yet, ironically, he's with me all the time.

This evening, it is my task to prepare a brief speech to be delivered at the memorial scheduled for tomorrow morning at my husband's school.

When I arrived home from work earlier this evening, I found a message alerting me to a broadcast of Wayne Dyer, a man some might call a motivational speaker. I move toward the television. I find the show and there he is: my husband's favorite guide and inspiration…in my own home, virtually speaking, on this anniversary eve.

I had been struggling with my challenge to compose the right things to say, and now, thanks to this broadcast, the words flow from my heart onto the page…

In Memoriam—My thoughts five years after

Here we are, friends of this man who served this community for more than thirty years. We're in this building that he loved and cared for as if it were his own home. In so many ways, it was his home, and we can still feel his presence. He was devoted, as are we, who remember him.

Who can explain the ways in which life works with death and death with life? Who can do anything but assert one's will into the mystery of it and claim what belongs to one's experience? It is up to each of us to decide how we want death to be, what we want it to mean, what it can hold for our own life. It is up to each of us to claim what is ours about the whole affair of having and losing, about knowing and not knowing, and about doing the best we can with our spirit and imagination. We are creative beings, and we must do what we are here to do. And those of us who recognize this also recognize each other and find ways to cross-fertilize and affect our world so that we can create consciousness and thereby enrich the quality of our humanity.

This man we remember today was a high-quality humanitarian. A man who worked on himself, questioned himself, and refined himself until the day he died.

My husband admired Wayne Dyer. It was a kind of mentoring relationship in which he chose Wayne as a beacon in the ocean of tumultuous feeling that was the interior psyche of my deep and glorious man. The triumph of spirit over the daily difficulty of the human dilemma motivated both of them, and, resonating to what felt "true," my husband allowed himself to be influenced and shaped by another who speaks of simply channeling what he believes to be "the source of love, beauty, and creativity."

Is this a perfect way to spend the eve of the five-year anniversary of my husband's death? I get comfortable on the couch and allow myself to be soothed with the philosophy of intentionality, the power of intention as Wayne Dyer named his presentation. And I settle into the sermon-like comfort of a memorial service in my own home according to the principles they both held so dear.

Creativity, kindness, love, expansiveness, appreciation, and gratitude: Wayne Dyer speaks of these qualities as a reminder to me of my husband's life. I can remember him bending kindly to the smallest child, imbuing that moment with respect, and providing the space to nurture whatever was there to grow. That was his modus operandi: nurturing whatever could possibly grow and creating the conditions for that growth to continue. Wayne Dyer used the term "radical humility," and this is what Richard's daily posture embodied, the one we have all come to recall so clearly.

We all remember that gracious posture of a large man of great stature, a man of substance possessing a body language that invited esteem and growth by radiating the warmth of his smile and his expansive, tender soul. He was a sun, a radiator of loving light, a generator of a special quality of kindness that could make a giant difference in a tiny child's day.

He has touched us all deeply. We are fortunate to have his spirit surrounded by this sturdy school, which stands as a symbol of commitment to the blossoming of life, a caring and enduring community that honors and remembers him. And after all is said and done, all that we are is what is remembered of us.

Epilogue

*"...After all is said and done, all that we
are is what is remembered of us."*

What follows is my offering about how to find your
own "landing lights," and how to bring your own
voyage of despair and discovery safely to the next
level.

In closing this manuscript, and in searching for
passages that might make sense, I've decided to talk
about the process of giving ourselves permission. It
is my hope that the sum total of my experience of

widowhood may offer some validation for your own forays into the tremulous territory of life and love after Love.

When you lose money, you might think about ways to get it back. When you lose a limb, you might seek any number of ways to compensate for that loss.

When you lose Love, you may ask deeper questions. If loving another were a satisfying state of being and way of living, it would be inevitable to desire that feeling and need to experience that sense of connection again.

For me, the essential first step was to allow myself to fall in love with Love again. And that included my surroundings: my cats, my garden, my friendships, and my every human contact. What I craved was communion with the "Divine," a way of embracing Life itself with my heart open, unafraid of being wounded. This kind of willingness to risk pain was my choice, and it must be yours if you can ever give and receive intimate love again. As a psychologist, I know this to be true, and as a mature woman, I find it even more so.

That cycle of feeling the emptiness and filling the emptiness; the ambivalence of living with the void and risking the vulnerability of attachment after radical detachment—these are phases you must traverse as you reclaim your wholeness. And these are some of the questions you may ask:

- ❧ Is healing possible?
- ❧ What does it take to heal?
- ❧ What do I need, as an individual, so that I can heal?
- ❧ How much am I affected by my perceptions about how the outside world judges me?
- ❧ Who am I at my essence?
- ❧ What am I really about?
- ❧ How do I see and therefore live my identity?
- ❧ How can I create what I need for myself?

For me, as an extrovert, my journey takes me deep into myself through the lens of relationship. It's just who I am and who I have always been. (You may work differently.) My understanding of myself has emerged over a lifetime of interaction with others, whether through my family and its complexities, through my avid reading adventures as a child, or through my personality and its tendencies, through my choices and their consequences.

Because life keeps shifting even as we cling in trepidation to our quaking world, I knew instinctively that it was critical for me to learn to trust my own inclinations once again, to say yes to what Life offered as it pulled me magnetically back into its design. The rhythms of stillness and stimulation, the back and forth, the ebb and flow—these dislodged me from my self-protective chrysalis, like a butterfly caught in a tangle of leaves on the muddy bank of a stream, the movement of wind and water inviting me back into the dance of being alive.

"What about sex?" you may be wondering.

And you have every reason and right to ask. There is no greater affirmation of being alive and no one who has not pondered the question. The quandaries that arise are often riddled with themes of rightness, conventionality, appropriateness, timing, and the place of your heart in all of this.

In my own case, I found myself simultaneously drawn to and yet repelled by the dilemma until a trusted and enduring friendship helped me gain some comfort with the idea, and our authentic affection led us to a transitional experience that formed a necessary bridge between the territory of sacred marriage and the new, uncharted land of Virgin Widowhood. (For you, it might be different.)

This focus on sex and your vision of yourself as desirable and desiring, though daunting, is just one of many rites of passage that you will go through on your way to whatever is your own personal "Next."

Though travel, dining out, and decision-making may seem less shocking, you can feel equally lost and vulnerable as every first is somehow accomplished.

It my case, when Life presented me with this huge rupture in the fabric of my world, I was frozen. I experienced the anger that comes with feeling derailed. I yielded to the reality and surrendered to the experience, sometimes kicking and screaming, other times acting passive and listless. I quarantined myself. I licked my wounds. I slept and dreamed and walked in nature. I tried to orient myself by seeking the resonance, comfort, and interpretation of the earth. Through the company of other pilgrims on the path, I sought and found perspective.

At first, unlocking myself and letting Life in smarted like salt in a wound. And then the stinging ceased, and the healing began. It was imperceptible at first (which for an impatient person is the hardest part) and then in discernible ways—ways that really seem to make a difference in mood and outlook. I began—with relief and surprise—to catch myself feeling "normal" again.

It is natural for me to catalogue and collate emotions and events and finally to weave a story that makes sense and gives meaning to what has occurred. I always aim to give back, to locate others in need, to gather a group of fellow seekers, and to lead expeditions into the heart of the matter. This is what I did in January of the next year, the new century. This is how I moved on.

Borrowing from the spirit of the time and the synchronicity that was there for the taking, I engineered the gathering of twelve women and held a retreat to share in the soup of personal transformation. For a period of four mid-winter days, we sequestered ourselves by the sea, sharing stories, sustenance, sisterhood, and the alchemy of science, art, and visions to move us forward on our respective paths.

It is notable that to this day, the experience of that particular confluence of personalities continues to connect us. In truth, we rode the waves of that combined experience into the "Next" of each of our lives, and we actually still do. Timing can be everything.

And so, dear reader, I wish to leave you with an affirmation of your own power to heal and choose. Your own depths are fertile, your tears will soften your soul, and your solace will emerge from the fact that you are inextricably connected to an array of elements and seasons—your own and those of the world.

When loss and severance render us out of step with the world, the pain and isolation that we feel can seem impossible to breach. What you can take with you from this work is the knowledge that you have the resources and the ability to connect with others and to reconnect with the source of all creativity.

You are made of paired opposites, and those combinations seal your complexity and thus your ability to make gains out of losses. To utilize the uniqueness of your humanity is to be part of a magical and universal force capable of that kind of creative transformation.

I walk this life with my eyes open and sandals on my feet. I carry little with me and use what I can from along the way. I am walking the dusty path from one shore of an island, to the next.

It always feels to me as though I'm navigating some topography...life as a hike, so to speak. And so it goes, experience after experience, moment after moment, putting one foot in front of the other. We keep going. We keep making the best of each chance to climb the ladder out into a new life. To stay in the old life would have been to choose a life with a hole in it, rather than to revise the plan and be whole in it. I chose the latter.

And the choice was not—*is* not—without consequence. I haven't been able to hold onto everything as much as I may have wanted to. Instead, I have experienced the rush of letting go. Later, if it is meant to be, some dropped stitches will find their way back into the fabric of my life.

Within these interwoven transitions, we make sacrifices. I have had to let go of certain things: friendships, plenty of acquaintances, a number of activities, certain financial comforts, and many self-serving routines. And so it goes: adding and subtracting, sorting and arranging, choosing and surrendering.

There were dreams to release as well, the very tension that holds a life together. To have my own work continues to be a life raft, a craft that spins wheat into gold. And today—still—the work of understanding the grieving process, and the life identity that was, is balanced by my hunger for meaningful experiences...spirits of adventure and an openness of mind.

The art and action of journal keeping have helped focus the metaphor of "journey" before me. Each moment, recalled and renamed, elevates the experience to its true value, like a pebble on the path upon which to tread the unknown territory. My words conspire to make the unknown familiar and friendly, a most subjective map of one woman's experience as a "virgin" widow.

The real test of a life, it seems to me, is how you learn and grow. With each day, your life will unfold like petals if you permit it to do so—if you welcome it and say yes and stay open—you will experience the pleasure of peace and the recovery that is your birthright. Light is all around if you can let go and let it in.

With a sacred place in my heart forever devoted to cherish the man I was blessed to know, irresistible life now animates and nourishes my soul, leading me where it will.

Dear Reader: What remains to be said about grief?

For me, when the question is asked, I always have the same image: a dark and convoluted cave with different textures on the wall, so dark so that you cannot see around corners. The walls, sensed and felt with your hands and tentatively with your feet, are sometimes so sharp as to cut like tiny blades, sometimes so splintery as you explore, and you're left with no choice but to have shards of glass embedded in your exploring fingers. And then there's the wetness, the surprising pools of water at your feet and the slippery dampness on your cheeks. It's a journey through your own underground, the landscape ever changing: twisty-turny, narrow, and compressed.

And there are times that it opens into more spaciousness—"rooms"—that give us pause, maybe even a little relief, and some perspective. Maybe even a platform of some sort upon which to perch for a while.

Grief is labyrinth like. Obsessive. It goes back and forth over the same territory: from differing heights and depths, ultimately in varying shades of increasing light and height and width until finally, one day, there's that suggestion of light coming from an unknown source that this gradually draws you to it. And then it's undeniable. You see some possibility illuminated, sense some shift; you receive the blessed ability to see again, and that itself carries its own challenge because the upside of the darkness is the solitude and protection of being tightly held.

Epilogue

Grief can be resolved, dissolved. But there's one prerequisite: You have to be willing to move on— not run away – but move on through the disturbing lessons that loss inevitably delivers.

To metabolize those lessons, you need to have a concept of life, a kind of philosophy of life. Not so much knowing what it's about, but knowing that it is a chain of discoveries, both linear and circular/ spiraling. And that without a concept like this to guide you, you're a body without a skeleton and you are likely to grow in on yourself, to become involuted as well as convoluted. At the very least this is extraordinarily painful – for it is both a psychical and physical death sentence as well.

For without some structure to guide us, we naturally feel lost. At best, we are lost in the moment, which can be the domain of productive creativity, or at worst, wandering and wondering, staving off the terrifying void that is lurking just outside the borders of your imagination.

So, I offer my journey as a straw man, something to bounce off, not as a prescription or advice, but rather as another story that holds elements that when you touch them, like phosphorous, or shake them, they light up; they shed light. I invite you to play with them—to take them from where they are to where they might apply to your life. They're simply light-buds ... tools only in the sense that they give you something to hold onto. Keep or throw them away; toss them in the air and see what they do. Dance with them. Share them with others.

Pebbles,
these moments of substance
these moments of truth
"Look!"
I can have the one that I can name
Naming the substance
Telling the truth
Becomes a pebble
A pebble dropped
respectfully where it lands
Being what it is
it forms
a dot!
Connect these dots
you have a path...
a path of
pebbles.

Andrea Gould-Marks

Tucson, Arizona

March 2012

Andrea Gould-Marks now resides in Tucson, Arizona, where she continues the evolution of her work on change and transition with special focus on grief and loss.

For more information, to connect directly with Andrea, and to order from her portfolio of learning tools, please visit www.lucidlearning. com/virginwidow.

58577605R00105

Made in the USA
Charleston, SC
13 July 2016